PHP AND MYSQL WEB DEVELOPMENT

A Practical Guide to Building Dynamic Websites and Databases

THOMPSON CARTER

TABLE OF CONTENTS

INTRODUCTION

INTRODUCTION

Introduction to "PHP and MySQL Web Development"

The Importance of PHP and MySQL in Modern Web Development

In today's digital landscape, web development has become a cornerstone of countless industries, from small startups to major tech giants. At the heart of this web evolution lies a powerful duo: PHP and MySQL. Despite the rise of new frameworks and languages, PHP remains one of the most widely used server-side scripting languages, powering nearly 80% of websites, including some of the most popular platforms globally, like Facebook and Wikipedia. Similarly, MySQL has established itself as a premier relational database management system, essential for storing and managing large volumes of data for millions of users worldwide.

But what makes PHP and MySQL such enduring and effective tools for web development? At their core, both are open-source technologies, which means they're freely available and consistently improved by a vibrant community of developers. This collaborative foundation keeps them up-to-date with industry standards and innovations, making them highly flexible and adaptable. In other words, PHP and MySQL are here to stay—and learning them opens doors to a wide range of career opportunities and personal projects.

For budding web developers, mastering PHP and MySQL is an ideal way to understand how data-driven web applications work. PHP handles the server-side logic, interacting with databases, managing user sessions, and processing requests, while MySQL handles the complex data storage and retrieval processes in the background. Together, these technologies form a comprehensive toolkit for creating dynamic, interactive websites that can scale to accommodate user growth and data expansion.

Who This Book is For

This book is crafted with accessibility in mind. Whether you're a novice just getting your start in web development, an intermediate developer looking to add server-side skills to your repertoire, or an entrepreneur who wants to build and maintain your own web applications, this guide will serve you well.

Beginners: If you're starting with a limited background in programming, this book will introduce you to the essentials of PHP and MySQL in a clear, step-by-step manner. We'll avoid heavy jargon, focusing instead on real-world examples that make the learning process enjoyable and relatable.

Intermediate Developers: Maybe you've already worked with front-end languages like HTML, CSS, and JavaScript, or even other backend languages. This book will guide you through PHP and MySQL in a way that enhances your existing skills, enabling you to build full-stack applications and tackle a wider range of development tasks.

Aspiring Web Developers and Entrepreneurs: For those with an entrepreneurial spirit, knowing how to create and manage a website can be an invaluable asset. This book provides the tools and techniques to help you build your own platform, blog, e-commerce site, or any other web-based project you have in mind.

What Readers Will Learn

With a hands-on, example-driven approach, this book aims to teach you both the "how" and the "why" behind PHP and MySQL. Throughout the chapters, you'll find that each concept is paired with practical applications. By the end of this book, you'll have created your own database-driven web applications and learned best practices to maintain them.

Here's a snapshot of the skills you'll acquire:

1. **Setting up a Development Environment**: You'll start with the basics, setting up PHP, MySQL, and a local server environment on your machine, so you can follow along with the examples and projects.
2. **Mastering PHP and SQL Syntax**: From variables and loops to functions and arrays, you'll gain a solid understanding of PHP syntax and how to write efficient SQL queries to interact with your database.

3. **Building Interactive Forms**: Forms are integral to web applications, and you'll learn how to build and process forms in PHP, allowing users to submit information that can be stored and accessed later.

4. **Connecting PHP with MySQL**: This book will guide you on how to make PHP and MySQL work together seamlessly. You'll learn how to retrieve, insert, update, and delete data in your database.

5. **Creating a User Authentication System**: As one of the book's highlights, you'll develop a secure login and registration system, complete with sessions and cookies, so users can have personalized experiences on your site.

6. **Understanding Object-Oriented PHP**: Once you've mastered the basics, you'll move on to object-oriented programming (OOP) concepts, which are essential for building larger applications.

7. **Developing a Content Management System (CMS)**: By the end, you'll build a basic CMS that can handle multiple users, articles, and comments—a valuable asset if you plan to create or manage a website with frequently updated content.

Tools and Setup Guide

Before diving into code, setting up your environment properly is crucial. Don't worry if this sounds technical—this book will walk you through each step, ensuring you have the right tools and configurations in place.

Installing PHP and MySQL: You'll start by installing the software necessary to develop locally on your computer, with guidance on tools like XAMPP, MAMP, or WAMP, depending on your operating system. This installation gives you a local environment that mimics the functionality of a live server, so you can test and debug your code before deploying it.

Choosing the Right Code Editor: There are several code editors and integrated development environments (IDEs) tailored for PHP development. Visual Studio Code, PHPStorm, and Sublime Text are some popular options, each with features to enhance your coding experience. We'll explore how to set up these editors for maximum efficiency.

Basic Command-Line Usage: Understanding a few command-line basics can make development easier, especially when working with databases. This book provides an overview of commands you'll frequently use, from navigating directories to starting and stopping services.

Coding Conventions and Best Practices
In this book, we'll emphasize the importance of clean, readable, and secure code. Following coding conventions makes your code

easier to maintain and reduces the likelihood of errors. Here's a sneak peek of some practices we'll cover:

- **Consistent Naming Conventions**: Choosing clear, descriptive variable names improves readability and helps you, or others, understand your code at a glance.
- **Indentation and Formatting**: Organized, consistently indented code is more accessible and less prone to hidden errors. This book includes samples and best practices for clean code.
- **Code Comments**: Comments clarify complex sections of code and serve as reminders for future changes or bug fixes.

Security is another cornerstone of good development. As you'll learn, user input should always be validated to protect against common vulnerabilities like SQL injection and cross-site scripting (XSS). We'll address these risks in dedicated sections so that you feel confident building secure applications.

Overview of the Book Structure and Learning Path

This book's structure follows a logical path, starting from fundamental concepts and gradually introducing more complex ideas. Each chapter builds upon the last, ensuring you have a solid foundation before moving on. Here's how we'll progress:

- **Learning in Stages**: Each chapter covers a specific concept or skill, with examples that demonstrate its use in real-world scenarios.

- **Project-Based Exercises**: After learning a new concept, you'll have a chance to apply it through hands-on exercises. These projects are cumulative, so by the end of the book, you'll have a portfolio of mini-projects to showcase your skills.

- **Checkpoints for Skill Assessment**: To help you gauge your understanding, each chapter concludes with a review or test question. These checkpoints encourage you to revisit key ideas and consolidate your knowledge.

Why PHP and MySQL Are Worth Learning for the Future

The tech industry is ever-evolving, but PHP and MySQL continue to be widely used across the web. PHP's simplicity and versatility make it an ideal choice for small businesses, startups, and freelancers who want to build fast, effective solutions. Additionally, as PHP evolves with new features, such as those introduced in PHP 8, it becomes an increasingly powerful and efficient language.

MySQL's robustness and scalability, on the other hand, ensure it remains relevant for both small and large-scale applications. By learning these tools together, you're equipping yourself with skills that will be valuable in the industry for years to come.

CHAPTER 1: INTRODUCTION TO WEB DEVELOPMENT BASICS

What is Web Development?

Web development is the process of building and maintaining websites or web applications that are accessible over the internet or a private network. Websites are generally categorized into two types: *static* and *dynamic*.

- **Static Websites**: These are basic websites where the content remains the same for every visitor. Each page is a separate HTML file, and updates require manual changes to each file. Think of a simple "About Us" page with text and images.

- **Dynamic Websites**: These sites serve different content based on user interactions or data, which is where PHP and MySQL come in. Unlike static websites, dynamic websites pull content from a database, allowing for personalized user experiences, like shopping carts, user profiles, or dashboards.

Dynamic web development involves *client-side* and *server-side* technologies. The client-side is what users see in their browser (HTML, CSS, JavaScript), while the server-side handles data processing and interaction with databases (in this case, PHP and MySQL).

Why PHP and MySQL?

PHP (Hypertext Preprocessor) and MySQL (My Structured Query Language) are an ideal combination for building dynamic, data-driven websites. Here's why they're a great choice for beginners and professionals alike:

- **PHP**: As a server-side language, PHP enables you to create interactive and functional web applications. It is known for its simplicity, large support community, and compatibility with various systems and databases. It's the backbone of many popular platforms, like WordPress and Facebook.

- **MySQL**: A powerful relational database management system (RDBMS), MySQL is responsible for managing and retrieving data. It can store large amounts of structured data and is widely compatible with PHP. Together, PHP and MySQL allow you to create websites that store and access data easily, which is essential for modern web applications.

Setting Up a Local Server

To start developing in PHP and MySQL, we need to set up a local environment on your computer, simulating the environment of a live server. This allows you to code, test, and debug locally before deploying to a live server.

Step 1: Choosing Your Local Server Solution

There are several tools to help you set up a local server. Here are three popular options:

- **XAMPP**: Available for Windows, macOS, and Linux, XAMPP is a free, cross-platform server package that includes PHP, MySQL, and Apache (a web server) in a single package.
- **MAMP**: Primarily for macOS but also available for Windows, MAMP provides a straightforward solution for setting up a local server with PHP and MySQL.
- **WAMP**: For Windows users, WAMP provides a Windows-specific alternative with an easy interface to manage the server environment.

Step 2: Installing XAMPP (Example)

Let's use XAMPP as an example, as it's widely used and provides everything needed to get started with PHP and MySQL.

1. **Download XAMPP**: Go to Apache Friends and download the XAMPP version that corresponds to your operating system.
2. **Run the Installer**: Once downloaded, run the installer and follow the installation prompts. Ensure both Apache and MySQL are selected in the components section.

3. **Start the Server**: Open the XAMPP Control Panel and start the Apache and MySQL modules. If they turn green, your server is running, and you're ready to start developing.

4. **Accessing Localhost**: Open a web browser and enter http://localhost/ in the address bar. If XAMPP is correctly installed, you should see the XAMPP welcome page.

Step 3: Setting Up Your Development Directory

After installing XAMPP, you'll need a workspace where you can store your PHP files.

1. **Locate the htdocs Folder**: In the XAMPP installation directory (often C:\xampp\ on Windows), open the htdocs folder. This is your web root directory where you'll save all PHP files for development.

2. **Create a Test File**: To ensure PHP is working, create a file named test.php in the htdocs folder. Open this file in a text editor and add the following code:

php

```
<?php
echo "Hello, world!";
?>
```

3. **Run the Test File**: Open your browser and enter http://localhost/test.php. If your setup is correct, you'll see "Hello, world!" displayed on the page.

Step 4: Accessing phpMyAdmin

To manage your MySQL databases, XAMPP includes *phpMyAdmin*, a user-friendly web interface.

1. **Access phpMyAdmin**: In your browser, go to http://localhost/phpmyadmin/.
2. **Creating Your First Database**: Click on the *Databases* tab and enter a name for your new database. Click *Create*. You'll use this database for storing information in your PHP applications.

Building a Simple PHP and MySQL Application

Now that you have PHP and MySQL running, let's outline the steps for building a very basic application—a guestbook where users can leave messages.

1. **Creating the Database Table**:
   - In phpMyAdmin, select your database, click *SQL*, and run the following SQL query:

   sql

   CREATE TABLE guestbook (

id INT AUTO_INCREMENT PRIMARY KEY,

name VARCHAR(50),

message TEXT,

created_at   TIMESTAMP   DEFAULT
CURRENT_TIMESTAMP

);

2. This query creates a table named guestbook with columns for an ID, name, message, and timestamp.

3. **Writing the PHP Code**:

   o Create a new file in the htdocs folder called guestbook.php.

   o Write the PHP code to connect to the database, retrieve guestbook entries, and allow users to add new messages.

4. **Testing the Application**:

   o Open http://localhost/guestbook.php in your browser.

   o Add and view messages to ensure the application interacts with MySQL as expected.

This chapter introduced you to the basic setup and explained why PHP and MySQL are valuable for building dynamic, interactive websites. Now that you have a functioning local server, you're ready to dive into PHP basics in the next chapter, where you'll learn the syntax and foundational concepts necessary for more complex projects.

CHAPTER 2: GETTING STARTED WITH PHP

What is PHP?

PHP (Hypertext Preprocessor) is a server-side scripting language widely used for web development. Unlike HTML or JavaScript, which run on the client's browser, PHP runs on the server. When a user requests a PHP page, the server executes the PHP code, generates HTML output, and sends it back to the user's browser. This approach allows PHP to interact with databases, manage user sessions, and create personalized, dynamic content.

Here's an example of how PHP works in a web application:

1. A user submits a form on a website, triggering a request to a PHP file.
2. The server processes the PHP code, which may involve querying a database or validating data.
3. The PHP script generates HTML content based on the result.

4. The server sends the HTML output to the user's browser for display.

With PHP, developers can create content that changes based on user input, real-time data, or user behavior, making it an essential tool for interactive websites.

PHP Syntax Basics

Let's look at the basic syntax of PHP. PHP code is typically embedded within HTML, allowing you to mix static HTML content with dynamic PHP code.

```php
<!DOCTYPE html>
<html>
<head>
   <title>My First PHP Page</title>
</head>
<body>
   <h1>Welcome to PHP!</h1>
   <?php
      echo "Hello, world! This is my first PHP script.";
   ?>
</body>
</html>
```

In the example above, PHP code is placed inside <?php ... ?> tags. Anything between these tags is processed by the PHP interpreter on the server. The echo statement outputs text directly to the browser.

Comments in PHP

Comments are notes you can add to your code that won't be executed. They're useful for explaining what your code does, making it easier for you and others to understand.

- **Single-line comments**: Use // or # for single-line comments.
- **Multi-line comments**: Use /* ... */ for comments that span multiple lines.

php
```php
<?php
    // This is a single-line comment
    # Another single-line comment


    /* This is a
       multi-line comment */
?>
```

Variables in PHP

Variables in PHP are used to store data that can change during program execution. All PHP variables start with a $ sign, followed by the variable name.

Example of declaring variables:

php

```php
<?php
    $name = "John Doe";      // String
    $age = 25;               // Integer
    $is_student = true;      // Boolean
    $gpa = 3.75;             // Float
?>
```

Naming Rules for Variables:

- Variables must begin with a letter or an underscore.
- They cannot start with a number.
- Variable names are case-sensitive ($name and $Name are different).

Data Types in PHP

PHP supports several data types, each used for storing different kinds of information. Here's an overview:

1. **String**: A sequence of characters used to store text.

   php
   ```php
   $greeting = "Hello, World!";
   ```

2. **Integer**: A whole number (positive or negative).

   php

$year = 2023;

3. **Float (Double)**: A number with a decimal point.

php
$temperature = 98.6;

4. **Boolean**: A true or false value, commonly used in conditions.

php
$is_active = true;

5. **Array**: A collection of values stored in a single variable.

php
$colors = array("red", "blue", "green");

6. **Null**: A variable with a NULL value has no value assigned to it.

php
$user_name = null;

Working with Strings

Strings are a common data type, especially when displaying text on a website. You can manipulate strings in various ways:

- **Concatenation**: Join two or more strings using the . (dot) operator.

```php
$first_name = "John";
$last_name = "Doe";
echo $first_name . " " . $last_name;  // Outputs: John Doe
```

- **String Functions**: PHP provides several functions to manipulate strings.

```php
$str = "Hello, World!";
echo strlen($str);        // Outputs: 13
echo str_replace("World", "PHP", $str); // Outputs: Hello, PHP!
```

Basic Arithmetic Operations

PHP supports arithmetic operations such as addition, subtraction, multiplication, and division.

```php
<?php
  $x = 10;
  $y = 5;

  echo $x + $y;  // Addition: Outputs 15
```

```
echo $x - $y;  // Subtraction: Outputs 5
echo $x * $y;  // Multiplication: Outputs 50
echo $x / $y;  // Division: Outputs 2
?>
```

PHP also supports modulus (%) for finding the remainder and exponentiation (**).

Using PHP as a Server-Side Language

One of PHP's most powerful features is its ability to run on the server, process data, and generate HTML dynamically. Here's a practical example of using PHP to interact with a user through form data.

Example: Processing User Input

Let's create a simple form where users enter their name, and PHP displays a personalized message.

HTML Form:

```
html
<!DOCTYPE html>
<html>
<head>
   <title>PHP Form Example</title>
</head>
<body>
   <form action="welcome.php" method="post">
```

```
    Name: <input type="text" name="name">
    <input type="submit">
  </form>
</body>
</html>
```

PHP Script (welcome.php):

```php
php
<?php
  $name = $_POST['name'];
  echo "Hello, " . htmlspecialchars($name) . "!";
?>
```

Here's a breakdown:

1. **HTML Form**: This form uses the POST method to send data to welcome.php.

2. **PHP Script**: In welcome.php, the PHP code retrieves the name input using $_POST['name']. Using htmlspecialchars() prevents HTML injection attacks by converting special characters to HTML entities.

In this chapter, you learned the basics of PHP syntax, variables, and data types. You also saw how PHP can handle user input, making it ideal for creating interactive, dynamic websites. With this foundational knowledge, you're ready to explore more complex topics, such as control structures and working with arrays, in the upcoming chapters.

CHAPTER 3: UNDERSTANDING MYSQL FUNDAMENTALS

What is MySQL?

MySQL is one of the most popular open-source RDBMSs, widely used for managing databases in web applications. It's particularly well-suited for handling large amounts of structured data, making it an excellent choice for applications that require data storage, such as e-commerce websites, content management systems, and social networks.

MySQL uses SQL, a standardized language for querying and managing databases. SQL allows developers to retrieve, insert, update, and delete data with simple, structured commands. Paired with PHP, MySQL enables you to create applications where user data (like login credentials, posts, comments) is stored securely and retrieved as needed.

Setting Up MySQL

Before we can start working with MySQL, you'll need to set it up on your local server. If you're using XAMPP, MAMP, or WAMP, MySQL should already be included and ready to use.

1. **Start MySQL Server**: Open your server control panel (XAMPP, MAMP, or WAMP) and start the MySQL service.

2. **Accessing phpMyAdmin**: phpMyAdmin is a graphical interface for managing MySQL databases. Open a web browser and go to http://localhost/phpmyadmin/ to access it.

3. **Creating a Database**: In phpMyAdmin, click on the *Databases* tab, enter a name for your database (e.g., my_website), and click *Create*. This creates a new database that will hold all your tables and data.

Understanding Databases and Tables

In MySQL, a database is a container for organizing and storing related data, and within each database, data is structured into tables.

- **Database**: Think of a database as a file cabinet that holds all related information for your application.

- **Tables**: Tables are the individual files inside the cabinet, each storing a specific type of information (e.g., users, products, orders).

Each table is made up of **columns** (fields) and **rows** (records):

- **Columns**: Define the type of data stored (e.g., name, age, email).
- **Rows**: Represent individual entries within the table (e.g., each user's details).

Example: A users Table

Suppose you want to create a table to store user information. Here's what the structure might look like:

id name	email	age
1 John Doe	john@example.com	28
2 Jane Smith	jane@example.com	34

In this table:

- id is a unique identifier for each user (often the primary key).
- name, email, and age are additional fields holding user data.

Creating Tables in MySQL

In phpMyAdmin, let's create a table called users with fields for id, name, email, and age:

1. **Navigate to Your Database**: In phpMyAdmin, click on the my_website database.
2. **Create Table**: Enter users as the table name and specify the number of columns (4 in this case).
3. **Define Columns**:
   - id: INT, Primary Key, Auto Increment.
   - name: VARCHAR(50), allows up to 50 characters.
   - email: VARCHAR(100), allows up to 100 characters.
   - age: INT, integer value for storing age.
4. **Save**: Click *Save* to create the table.

This users table can now store information for each user, with each row representing one unique user.

Basic SQL Queries

SQL is the language used to interact with MySQL databases. Here are some basic SQL queries for adding, retrieving, updating, and deleting data in the users table.

1. **INSERT**: Adding Data to the Table

   The INSERT INTO statement is used to add new records to a table.

sql

```
INSERT INTO users (name, email, age) VALUES ('Alice Brown', 'alice@example.com', 30);
```

This query adds a new row to the users table with the name "Alice Brown", email "alice@example.com", and age 30.

2. **SELECT**: Retrieving Data from the Table

The SELECT statement is used to retrieve data from a table. You can use * to select all columns or specify individual columns.

sql

```
SELECT * FROM users;
```

This query retrieves all records from the users table. If you only want to retrieve names and emails, use:

sql

```
SELECT name, email FROM users;
```

3. **WHERE Clause**: Filtering Results

You can use the WHERE clause to filter records based on specific conditions.

sql

SELECT * FROM users WHERE age > 25;

This query retrieves all users older than 25.

4. **UPDATE**: Modifying Existing Data

The UPDATE statement allows you to modify existing records. Use the WHERE clause to specify which record(s) to update.

sql

UPDATE users SET email = 'newemail@example.com' WHERE id = 1;

This query updates the email address for the user with id equal to 1.

5. **DELETE**: Removing Data from the Table

The DELETE statement removes records from the table. Use the WHERE clause to specify which record(s) to delete.

sql

DELETE FROM users WHERE id = 2;

This query deletes the record with id equal to 2 from the users table.

6. **Primary Keys and Unique Constraints**

The id column in our users table is a **primary key**, meaning it uniquely identifies each row. Primary keys ensure that each record is unique, which is essential for maintaining data integrity. You can also apply **unique constraints** to other columns (e.g., email) if you need unique values in multiple fields.

Using SQL in PHP

To make PHP interact with MySQL, you'll often embed SQL queries within PHP scripts. Here's a quick example of how you might use PHP to insert a new user into the database.

PHP Code:

php

```php
<?php
$servername = "localhost";
$username = "root";
$password = "";
$dbname = "my_website";

// Create connection
$conn = new mysqli($servername, $username, $password, $dbname);
```

```php
// Check connection
if ($conn->connect_error) {
    die("Connection failed: " . $conn->connect_error);
}

// Insert data
$sql = "INSERT INTO users (name, email, age) VALUES ('Mark Twain', 'mark@example.com', 45)";

if ($conn->query($sql) === TRUE) {
    echo "New record created successfully";
} else {
    echo "Error: " . $sql . "<br>" . $conn->error;
}

$conn->close();
?>
```

This PHP code connects to the MySQL database and inserts a new row into the users table. It checks for a successful connection and confirms if the record was added.

In this chapter, we covered MySQL fundamentals: setting up MySQL, creating databases and tables, and using basic SQL queries. You now have the foundational knowledge to structure data using MySQL and interact with it through PHP. In the next chapter, we'll focus on integrating PHP and MySQL, enabling us to perform real-time data operations in web applications.

CHAPTER 4: INTEGRATING PHP AND MYSQL

Why Integrate PHP and MySQL?

By integrating PHP with MySQL, you can build web applications that handle user input, store it in a database, and display it dynamically. For example, a blog application could use PHP and MySQL to save blog posts to a database, retrieve them for display, and allow users to interact with each post. This approach is more efficient than creating a static HTML page for each piece of content, as it automates content handling and allows for data-driven interactivity.

Setting Up a PHP-MySQL Connection

To interact with MySQL from PHP, we need to establish a connection between the two. There are two primary ways to connect PHP with MySQL:

1. **MySQLi** (MySQL Improved) – an updated, object-oriented way to connect with MySQL.
2. **PDO (PHP Data Objects)** – a more flexible option that works with multiple database types.

In this chapter, we'll use **MySQLi** as it's specific to MySQL and widely used for PHP-MySQL integrations.

Establishing a MySQLi Connection

To connect PHP with a MySQL database using MySQLi, you need four pieces of information:

- **Hostname**: Often localhost if the database is on the same server.
- **Username**: Default is usually root for local servers.
- **Password**: Blank by default for local servers (though this should be set for security in production).
- **Database Name**: The name of the database you want to interact with.

Here's a simple script to establish a connection:

php

```php
<?php
$servername = "localhost";
$username = "root";
$password = "";
$dbname = "my_website";

// Create connection
$conn = new mysqli($servername, $username, $password, $dbname);

// Check connection
if ($conn->connect_error) {
    die("Connection failed: " . $conn->connect_error);
}
echo "Connected successfully";
?>
```

This script:

1. Creates a new mysqli object and attempts to connect to the database.
2. Checks for a connection error, and if successful, outputs "Connected successfully."

Running Basic MySQL Operations with PHP

Once the connection is established, we can use PHP to perform basic CRUD (Create, Read, Update, Delete) operations on the database.

1. Inserting Data (Create Operation)

To insert data into a MySQL table, you can use an INSERT INTO SQL query within your PHP script. Suppose we have a users table with columns name, email, and age.

PHP Script for Inserting Data:

```php
php
<?php
// Connection setup
$conn = new mysqli("localhost", "root", "", "my_website");

// Check connection
if ($conn->connect_error) {
    die("Connection failed: " . $conn->connect_error);
}

// Insert query
$name = "Alice";
$email = "alice@example.com";
$age = 25;
$sql = "INSERT INTO users (name, email, age) VALUES ('$name', '$email', $age)";
```

```php
if ($conn->query($sql) === TRUE) {
    echo "New record created successfully";
} else {
    echo "Error: " . $sql . "<br>" . $conn->error;
}

// Close connection
$conn->close();
?>
```

In this example:

- We use INSERT INTO to add a new user.
- The query() method executes the SQL statement, and we check if the operation was successful.
- Finally, we close the connection with $conn->close().

2. Retrieving Data (Read Operation)

To fetch data from a database, we use the SELECT statement. Suppose we want to retrieve all users in the users table.

PHP Script for Retrieving Data:

php

```php
<?php
$conn = new mysqli("localhost", "root", "", "my_website");
```

```php
// Check connection
if ($conn->connect_error) {
    die("Connection failed: " . $conn->connect_error);
}

$sql = "SELECT id, name, email, age FROM users";
$result = $conn->query($sql);

if ($result->num_rows > 0) {
    // Output data for each row
    while($row = $result->fetch_assoc()) {
        echo "ID: " . $row["id"]. " - Name: " . $row["name"]. " - Email: " . $row["email"]. " - Age: " . $row["age"]. "<br>";
    }
} else {
    echo "0 results";
}

$conn->close();
?>
```

In this example:

- We execute the SELECT query to retrieve all rows from the users table.

- If the query returns results, we use a while loop to display each row's data.
- $result->fetch_assoc() fetches each row as an associative array, allowing us to access column values by their names.

3. Updating Data (Update Operation)

To modify existing records, we use the UPDATE statement. Suppose we want to update a user's email based on their ID.

PHP Script for Updating Data:

php

```php
<?php
$conn = new mysqli("localhost", "root", "", "my_website");

// Check connection
if ($conn->connect_error) {
    die("Connection failed: " . $conn->connect_error);
}

$sql = "UPDATE users SET email='newemail@example.com' WHERE id=1";

if ($conn->query($sql) === TRUE) {
    echo "Record updated successfully";
} else {
```

```php
    echo "Error updating record: " . $conn->error;
}


$conn->close();
?>
```

In this example:

- The UPDATE query changes the email of the user with id 1.
- We check if the operation was successful and output a message.

4. Deleting Data (Delete Operation)

To remove records from a table, use the DELETE statement. Suppose we want to delete a user based on their ID.

PHP Script for Deleting Data:

php

```php
<?php
$conn = new mysqli("localhost", "root", "", "my_website");


// Check connection
if ($conn->connect_error) {
    die("Connection failed: " . $conn->connect_error);
}
```

```php
$sql = "DELETE FROM users WHERE id=2";

if ($conn->query($sql) === TRUE) {
    echo "Record deleted successfully";
} else {
    echo "Error deleting record: " . $conn->error;
}

$conn->close();
?>
```

In this example:

- The DELETE query removes the row where id is 2.
- We check the operation's success and output a message accordingly.

Securing Your Database Interactions

To protect against SQL injection attacks (where malicious users can manipulate SQL queries), always validate and sanitize user input. For example, instead of directly embedding variables into SQL queries, use **prepared statements** in PHP.

Example of Using Prepared Statements with MySQLi

Here's a safer way to insert data using prepared statements:

php

```php
<?php
$conn = new mysqli("localhost", "root", "", "my_website");

if ($conn->connect_error) {
    die("Connection failed: " . $conn->connect_error);
}

// Prepare and bind
$stmt = $conn->prepare("INSERT INTO users (name, email, age)
VALUES (?, ?, ?)");
$stmt->bind_param("ssi", $name, $email, $age);

// Set parameters and execute
$name = "Bob";
$email = "bob@example.com";
$age = 29;
$stmt->execute();

echo "New record created successfully";

$stmt->close();
$conn->close();
?>
```

In this example:

- $conn->prepare() prepares an SQL statement for execution.

- $stmt->bind_param("ssi", ...) binds the parameters to the SQL query, where "ssi" specifies the data types (string, string, integer).
- This method improves security by preventing SQL injection.

In this chapter, we covered how to connect PHP to MySQL using MySQLi, including basic CRUD operations for creating, retrieving, updating, and deleting data. We also introduced prepared statements for secure interactions with the database, which helps protect against SQL injection.

With this integration foundation, you're now ready to start building PHP applications that store and retrieve data from MySQL. In the next chapter, we'll look into HTML and CSS essentials for PHP developers, preparing you to create visually appealing and interactive pages for your users.

CHAPTER 5: HTML AND CSS ESSENTIALS FOR PHP DEVELOPERS

Introduction to HTML and CSS

HTML (HyperText Markup Language) and CSS (Cascading Style Sheets) are the foundation of web page structure and styling:

- **HTML**: The backbone of any web page, HTML defines the structure of your content. It uses tags (such as <p> for paragraphs, <h1> for headings) to arrange text, images, and other elements.

- **CSS**: CSS controls the visual presentation of HTML content. You use CSS to style elements (e.g., change colors, fonts, and layouts) and make the page look more appealing.

For PHP developers, mastering HTML and CSS is essential because PHP dynamically generates HTML, which is then sent to the client's browser. Knowing how to structure and style HTML within your PHP applications will improve your ability to create functional and attractive web pages.

HTML Essentials for PHP Developers

Let's start with the core HTML concepts every PHP developer should understand. These include the basic structure of an HTML document, essential tags, forms for user input, and linking HTML files with PHP.

Basic HTML Document Structure

Here's a basic HTML document structure:

html

```
<!DOCTYPE html>
<html lang="en">
<head>
  <meta charset="UTF-8">
  <meta name="viewport" content="width=device-width, initial-scale=1.0">
```

```
<title>My First PHP Page</title>
</head>
<body>
  <h1>Welcome to My PHP-Driven Website</h1>
  <p>This is a simple HTML structure generated with PHP.</p>
</body>
</html>
```

- **<!DOCTYPE html>**: Declares the document type as HTML5.
- **<html>**: Root element that contains the entire HTML document.
- **<head>**: Contains metadata about the document (e.g., title, character set).
- **<body>**: The main content area where visible elements (like text, images, forms) are placed.

PHP can dynamically generate HTML structures like this, allowing you to create pages based on user actions or database content.

Common HTML Tags

Here are some commonly used HTML tags every PHP developer should know:

- **Headings**: <h1> to <h6> for different levels of headings.
- **Paragraphs**: <p> for blocks of text.

- **Links**: <a href="URL">Link Text</a> to link to other pages or sites.
- **Images**: <img src="image.jpg" alt="Description"> to display images.
- **Lists**: <ul> (unordered list) and <ol> (ordered list) for bulleted and numbered lists.
- **Tables**: <table>, <tr>, <td>, and <th> to create tables.

These elements are essential for structuring your page content and will often be embedded within PHP scripts to display dynamic data.

Working with HTML Forms in PHP

Forms are a key component in interactive applications, enabling users to submit data that PHP can process. Here's a basic example of an HTML form:

html

```
<!DOCTYPE html>
<html lang="en">
<head>
   <meta charset="UTF-8">
   <title>Contact Form</title>
</head>
<body>
   <form action="process_form.php" method="POST">
      <label for="name">Name:</label>
```

```
    <input type="text" id="name" name="name" required>

    <label for="email">Email:</label>
    <input type="email" id="email" name="email" required>

    <label for="message">Message:</label>
    <textarea id="message" name="message"></textarea>

    <button type="submit">Submit</button>
  </form>
</body>
</html>
```

Key elements of this form:

- **<form action="process_form.php" method="POST">**: Specifies the PHP file that will handle the form data (process_form.php) and the HTTP method (POST).
- **<input type="text" name="name">**: An input field for the user's name. The name attribute is essential because PHP uses it to access the form data.
- **<button type="submit">**: Submits the form data to the server.

PHP can use the $_POST or $_GET superglobal arrays to retrieve form data and process it in process_form.php.

CSS Essentials for PHP Developers

CSS is used to make HTML visually appealing by controlling the layout, colors, fonts, and more. Here's a breakdown of key CSS concepts every PHP developer should know.

CSS Syntax Basics

CSS is written as a set of rules that apply styles to HTML elements. Here's an example:

css

```
body {
    background-color: #f0f0f0;
    font-family: Arial, sans-serif;
}

h1 {
    color: #333;
    text-align: center;
}

p {
    font-size: 16px;
    color: #666;
}
```

- **Selector**: Targets an HTML element (e.g., body, h1).

- **Property**: Defines what aspect of the element to style (e.g., color, font-size).
- **Value**: Sets the property's appearance (e.g., #333, 16px).

CSS Box Model

The box model is crucial for layout management. Every HTML element is treated as a box, with four key parts:

- **Content**: The actual text or image inside the element.
- **Padding**: Space between the content and the border.
- **Border**: The edge around the padding.
- **Margin**: Space outside the border, separating the element from others.

Example:

css

```
div {
    padding: 10px;
    border: 2px solid #000;
    margin: 15px;
}
```

CSS Layout Techniques

CSS provides multiple ways to layout elements on a page. Here are a few common techniques:

1. **Flexbox**: A layout model for aligning items in rows or columns.

   css

   ```
   .container {
       display: flex;
       justify-content: center;
       align-items: center;
   }
   ```

2. **Grid**: A more powerful layout system for creating complex, two-dimensional layouts.

   css

   ```
   .grid-container {
       display: grid;
       grid-template-columns: repeat(3, 1fr);
       gap: 10px;
   }
   ```

3. **Positioning**: Controls an element's location using static, relative, absolute, fixed, or sticky positioning.

Applying CSS to PHP-Generated HTML

To apply CSS to HTML generated by PHP, you can include an external CSS file in your PHP pages or embed CSS directly within the <style> tags.

Example of including external CSS in a PHP file:

php

```
<!DOCTYPE html>
<html lang="en">
<head>
   <meta charset="UTF-8">
   <title>Styled PHP Page</title>
   <link rel="stylesheet" href="styles.css">
</head>
<body>
   <h1>Welcome to My Styled PHP Page</h1>
   <p>This paragraph is styled with CSS.</p>
</body>
</html>
```

In this example, styles.css contains all CSS styles. PHP dynamically generates the HTML content, which is styled using the CSS file.

Integrating HTML, CSS, and PHP for a Dynamic Application

Let's walk through a simple example where PHP dynamically generates content within an HTML page styled with CSS. We'll create a small application that displays a list of users stored in a MySQL database.

Step 1: PHP Script for Retrieving Data (users.php)

php

```php
<?php
// Database connection
$conn = new mysqli("localhost", "root", "", "my_website");

if ($conn->connect_error) {
    die("Connection failed: " . $conn->connect_error);
}

$sql = "SELECT name, email FROM users";
$result = $conn->query($sql);
?>

<!DOCTYPE html>
<html lang="en">
<head>
    <meta charset="UTF-8">
    <title>User List</title>
    <link rel="stylesheet" href="styles.css">
</head>
```

```php
<body>
  <h1>User List</h1>
  <ul>
    <?php
    if ($result->num_rows > 0) {
      // Output each user
      while ($row = $result->fetch_assoc()) {
        echo "<li>" . htmlspecialchars($row["name"]) . " - " .
htmlspecialchars($row["email"]) . "</li>";
      }
    } else {
      echo "<p>No users found.</p>";
    }
    $conn->close();
    ?>
  </ul>
</body>
</html>
```

In this example:

- PHP retrieves data from the users table in MySQL and dynamically generates a list of users within an HTML unordered list.
- CSS styling is added via an external file (styles.css), making it easy to control the presentation separately.

Step 2: CSS Styles for the Page (styles.css)

css

```css
body {
    font-family: Arial, sans-serif;
    background-color: #f9f9f9;
    color: #333;
}

h1 {
    color: #0056b3;
    text-align: center;
}

ul {
    list-style-type: none;
    padding: 0;
}

li {
    background-color: #e3f2fd;
    margin: 5px 0;
    padding: 10px;
    border: 1px solid #90caf9;
    border-radius: 5px;
```

}

The CSS file styles the list of users, giving each item a background color, border, and padding. This separation of content (HTML), style (CSS), and logic (PHP) is a best practice, making the application easy to maintain and visually appealing.

In this chapter, we covered HTML and CSS basics essential for PHP developers, including document structure, forms, and styling with CSS. We also demonstrated how PHP can dynamically generate HTML content styled with CSS, giving you the tools to create visually attractive and interactive web applications. Next, we'll dive into generating dynamic content with PHP, taking your applications to the next level by making them responsive to user input and database data.

CHAPTER 6: DYNAMIC CONTENT WITH PHP

What is Dynamic Content?
Dynamic content refers to web page elements that change based on user interactions, database queries, or other inputs. Unlike static content, which remains the same each time a page is loaded, dynamic content is updated as users interact with the application. This interactivity is essential for features like user profiles, news feeds, product listings, and more.

For example:

- An e-commerce site displays product details based on the user's search query.
- A blog retrieves and displays posts from a database, updating the content whenever a new post is added.

In this chapter, we'll explore how PHP retrieves data from a MySQL database and displays it dynamically, as well as how to handle user input for customization.

Retrieving and Displaying Data from a Database

To display dynamic content, you'll first need data stored in a MySQL database. Let's assume you have a database named my_website with a products table containing information about products.

Here's an example products table structure:

id	name	description	price	category
1	Laptop	High-performance laptop	1200	Electronics
2	Phone	Smartphone with advanced features	800	Electronics
3	Coffee Maker	Automatic coffee brewing machine	150	Kitchen

With PHP, you can retrieve this data and display it on a webpage. Let's walk through the steps.

Step 1: Setting Up the Database Connection

To retrieve data from MySQL, you'll first need to establish a connection. Here's a basic script to connect to the database:

php

```php
<?php
$servername = "localhost";
$username = "root";
$password = "";
$dbname = "my_website";


// Create connection
$conn = new mysqli($servername, $username, $password, $dbname);


// Check connection
if ($conn->connect_error) {
    die("Connection failed: " . $conn->connect_error);
}
?>
```

This script connects to the database using mysqli, and if successful, it allows PHP to interact with the my_website database.

Step 2: Retrieving Data with SQL Queries

Let's retrieve the list of products from the products table and display them on a webpage. Here's a PHP script that fetches all products and displays them in a simple HTML table.

php

```php
<?php
// Include the database connection code
$conn = new mysqli("localhost", "root", "", "my_website");

if ($conn->connect_error) {
    die("Connection failed: " . $conn->connect_error);
}

// Fetch products from the database
$sql = "SELECT id, name, description, price, category FROM products";
$result = $conn->query($sql);
?>

<!DOCTYPE html>
<html lang="en">
<head>
    <meta charset="UTF-8">
    <title>Product List</title>
```

```
</head>
<body>
    <h1>Product List</h1>
    <table border="1">
        <tr>
            <th>ID</th>
            <th>Name</th>
            <th>Description</th>
            <th>Price</th>
            <th>Category</th>
        </tr>
        <?php
        if ($result->num_rows > 0) {
            // Output data for each row
            while ($row = $result->fetch_assoc()) {
                echo "<tr>";
                echo "<td>" . htmlspecialchars($row["id"]) . "</td>";
                echo "<td>" . htmlspecialchars($row["name"]) . "</td>";
                echo "<td>" . htmlspecialchars($row["description"]) .
"</td>";
                echo "<td>" . htmlspecialchars($row["price"]) . "</td>";
                echo "<td>" . htmlspecialchars($row["category"]) .
"</td>";
                echo "</tr>";
            }
```

```
    } else {
        echo "<tr><td colspan='5'>No products found.</td></tr>";
    }
    $conn->close();
    ?>
  </table>
</body>
</html>
```

Explanation:

- The SQL query SELECT id, name, description, price, category FROM products retrieves all products from the products table.
- PHP's while loop displays each row of data as a table row (<tr>) in HTML.
- htmlspecialchars() is used to prevent HTML injection by converting special characters to HTML entities.

When you run this script, it outputs a table with a list of products from the database. This is a simple example of using PHP to display dynamic content retrieved from MySQL.

Handling User Input to Display Customized Content

Dynamic content often changes based on user input. For example, a search feature allows users to find specific products by name. In

PHP, you can retrieve and display filtered data based on what the user inputs.

Let's add a search form that enables users to search for products by name.

1. **HTML Form for Search Input**:

    html

    ```html
    <form action="search.php" method="GET">
        <label for="search">Search Products:</label>
        <input type="text" id="search" name="search" required>
        <button type="submit">Search</button>
    </form>
    ```

2. **PHP Script to Process Search Query (search.php)**:

    php

    ```php
    <?php
    // Database connection
    $conn = new mysqli("localhost", "root", "", "my_website");

    if ($conn->connect_error) {
        die("Connection failed: " . $conn->connect_error);
    ```

```php
}

// Get the search term from the user input
$searchTerm = $_GET['search'];

// Query to search for products with names matching the
search term
$sql = "SELECT id, name, description, price, category
FROM products WHERE name LIKE ?";
$stmt = $conn->prepare($sql);
$searchTerm = "%" . $searchTerm . "%";
$stmt->bind_param("s", $searchTerm);
$stmt->execute();
$result = $stmt->get_result();
?>
```

```html
<!DOCTYPE html>
<html lang="en">
<head>
    <meta charset="UTF-8">
    <title>Search Results</title>
</head>
<body>
    <h1>Search Results</h1>
    <table border="1">
```

```php
<tr>
    <th>ID</th>
    <th>Name</th>
    <th>Description</th>
    <th>Price</th>
    <th>Category</th>
</tr>
<?php
if ($result->num_rows > 0) {
    while ($row = $result->fetch_assoc()) {
        echo "<tr>";
        echo "<td>" . htmlspecialchars($row["id"]) . "</td>";
        echo "<td>" . htmlspecialchars($row["name"]) . "</td>";
        echo "<td>" . htmlspecialchars($row["description"]) . "</td>";
        echo "<td>" . htmlspecialchars($row["price"]) . "</td>";
        echo "<td>" . htmlspecialchars($row["category"]) . "</td>";
        echo "</tr>";
    }
} else {
```

```
        echo      "<tr><td      colspan='5'>No      results
found.</td></tr>";
    }
    $stmt->close();
    $conn->close();
    ?>
  </table>
</body>
</html>
```

Explanation:

- The HTML form sends a GET request to search.php, including the user's search term.

- In search.php, we retrieve the search term using $_GET['search'].

- The SQL query SELECT ... FROM products WHERE name LIKE ? finds products with names matching the search term.

- We use prepared statements ($stmt->prepare() and $stmt->bind_param()) to prevent SQL injection attacks, ensuring the search term is safely incorporated into the query.

- The search results are displayed in a table, similar to the previous example.

This dynamic interaction allows users to enter a search term and see the filtered product list in real time.

Using Dynamic Content to Display User-Specific Data

Dynamic content can also display user-specific data, such as user profiles, order histories, or account details. For example, if a user logs into an e-commerce site, PHP and MySQL can pull their order history from the database and display it on their profile page.

Here's a simplified example of displaying user-specific content based on a session variable:

1. **Starting a Session and Setting User Data**:

   php

```php
<?php
session_start();
$_SESSION['user_id'] = 1; // Example user ID for demonstration
?>
```

2. **Retrieving and Displaying User-Specific Data**:

   php

```php
<?php
session_start();
$userId = $_SESSION['user_id'];
```

```php
$conn = new mysqli("localhost", "root", "", "my_website");

if ($conn->connect_error) {
    die("Connection failed: " . $conn->connect_error);
}


// Fetch user-specific orders based on session user ID
$sql = "SELECT order_id, product_name, order_date FROM orders WHERE user_id = ?";
$stmt = $conn->prepare($sql);
$stmt->bind_param("i", $userId);
$stmt->execute();
$result = $stmt->get_result();
?>


<h1>Your Order History</h1>
<table border="1">
    <tr>
        <th>Order ID</th>
        <th>Product Name</th>
        <th>Order Date</th>
    </tr>
    <?php
    while ($row = $result->fetch_assoc()) {
        echo "<tr>";
```

```
        echo "<td>" . htmlspecialchars($row["order_id"]) .
"</td>";
        echo                        "<td>"                        .
htmlspecialchars($row["product_name"]) . "</td>";
        echo "<td>" . htmlspecialchars($row["order_date"]) .
"</td>";
        echo "</tr>";
    }
    $stmt->close();
    $conn->close();
    ?>
</table>
```

In this example:

- PHP retrieves the user_id from the session and uses it in an SQL query to fetch the user's order history.
- The query results are displayed as a table on the page, showing personalized content based on the user's login session.

In this chapter, you learned how to use PHP to display dynamic content, both by retrieving data from a MySQL database and by handling user input to customize what's displayed. With these skills, you can build interactive applications that display relevant information to users in real-time. In the next chapter, we'll look at creating and processing forms with PHP, enabling more complex user interactions, such as creating accounts, submitting comments, and more.

CHAPTER 7: FORMS AND USER INTERACTION

Introduction to Forms in Web Development

Forms are a primary way for users to interact with a website. When users fill out a form and submit it, the data they enter is sent to the server for processing. PHP can then take this data, perform actions based on it, and respond with a customized result. Forms are crucial for features such as:

- User registration and login systems
- Search queries
- Contact forms
- Surveys and feedback forms

In HTML, forms are created using the <form> element and various input elements, such as <input>, <textarea>, <select>, and <button>.

HTML Form Structure

Let's start with a simple form where users can submit their name and email address.

html

```
<!DOCTYPE html>
<html lang="en">
<head>
    <meta charset="UTF-8">
    <title>Simple Form</title>
</head>
<body>
    <h1>Sign Up</h1>
    <form action="process_form.php" method="POST">
        <label for="name">Name:</label>
        <input type="text" id="name" name="name" required>

        <label for="email">Email:</label>
        <input type="email" id="email" name="email" required>

        <button type="submit">Submit</button>
```

```
</form>
</body>
</html>
```

Explanation:

- **<form action="process_form.php" method="POST">**: The action attribute specifies the PHP file that will handle the form data, and the method attribute specifies how the data will be sent (here, as a POST request).

- **<input type="text">** and **<input type="email">**: These are form fields where users enter information. Each input has a name attribute, which PHP uses to identify the data.

- **<button type="submit">**: This button submits the form data to the specified PHP file.

Handling GET and POST Requests in PHP

In PHP, form data can be sent to the server using either the GET or POST method.

- **GET**: Data is appended to the URL as query parameters. It's best for non-sensitive data, such as search queries, since it can be seen in the URL.

- **POST**: Data is sent in the request body, making it more secure than GET. It's generally used for submitting forms with sensitive data, such as passwords or personal information.

GET Request Example

Here's an example of using GET to submit a search query.

1. **HTML Form for Search Query**:

html

```html
<form action="search.php" method="GET">
    <label for="query">Search:</label>
    <input type="text" id="query" name="query" required>
    <button type="submit">Search</button>
</form>
```

2. **PHP Code to Handle the GET Request (search.php)**:

php

```php
<?php
// Retrieve the search query from the URL
if (isset($_GET['query'])) {
    $query = $_GET['query'];
    echo "You searched for: " . htmlspecialchars($query);
} else {
    echo "No search query provided.";
}
?>
```

In this example:

- The form uses the GET method, so the query appears in the URL as ?query=yoursearchterm.
- $_GET['query'] retrieves the search term entered by the user.
- htmlspecialchars() is used to prevent HTML injection attacks.

POST Request Example

Let's process the Sign Up form using POST to submit the user's name and email.

1. **HTML Form (from earlier example)**:

html
```
<form action="process_form.php" method="POST">
    <label for="name">Name:</label>
    <input type="text" id="name" name="name" required>

    <label for="email">Email:</label>
    <input type="email" id="email" name="email" required>

    <button type="submit">Submit</button>
</form>
```

2. **PHP Code to Handle the POST Request (process_form.php)**:

php

```php
<?php
if ($_SERVER["REQUEST_METHOD"] == "POST") {
    // Retrieve and sanitize form data
    $name = htmlspecialchars($_POST['name']);
    $email = htmlspecialchars($_POST['email']);

    echo "Thank you, $name! Your email address $email has been recorded.";
} else {
    echo "Invalid request.";
}
?>
```

Explanation:

- We use $_SERVER["REQUEST_METHOD"] to check if the request method is POST.
- $_POST['name'] and $_POST['email'] retrieve the data submitted by the user.
- htmlspecialchars() is used to escape special characters, helping to secure the data.

Using POST keeps the submitted data hidden from the URL, making it more suitable for handling sensitive information.

Validating and Securing Form Data

User input should always be validated and sanitized to ensure data integrity and security. This helps protect your application from common security vulnerabilities, such as cross-site scripting (XSS) and SQL injection.

Validation Techniques

Validation ensures that data meets specific criteria before processing it. Here are some examples of common validations:

1. **Required Fields**: Check that required fields are not empty.

    php

    ```php
    if (empty($name)) {
        echo "Name is required.";
    }
    ```

2. **Email Validation**: Use PHP's filter_var() function to validate email addresses.

    php

    ```php
    if (!filter_var($email, FILTER_VALIDATE_EMAIL)) {
        echo "Invalid email format.";
    }
    ```

3. **Length Check**: Ensure that data does not exceed a certain length.

php

```
if (strlen($name) > 50) {
    echo "Name is too long.";
}
```

Sanitizing Input Data

Sanitizing data removes or escapes characters that could interfere with SQL queries or HTML. PHP provides functions for sanitization, such as:

- **htmlspecialchars()**: Converts special characters into HTML entities, preventing HTML injection.

  php

  ```
  $name = htmlspecialchars($name);
  ```

- **filter_var()**: Can be used with FILTER_SANITIZE_STRING to remove unwanted characters.

  php

```php
$email = filter_var($email, FILTER_SANITIZE_EMAIL);
```

Storing Form Data in a Database

Let's modify the signup form to save the submitted data to a MySQL database. Assume we have a users table with columns id, name, and email.

1. **PHP Script to Process and Store Form Data (save_user.php)**:

php

```php
<?php
// Database connection
$conn = new mysqli("localhost", "root", "", "my_website");

if ($conn->connect_error) {
    die("Connection failed: " . $conn->connect_error);
}

if ($_SERVER["REQUEST_METHOD"] == "POST") {
    // Sanitize and validate input
    $name = htmlspecialchars($_POST['name']);
    $email = filter_var($_POST['email'], FILTER_SANITIZE_EMAIL);
```

```php
    if (!filter_var($email, FILTER_VALIDATE_EMAIL)) {
        echo "Invalid email format.";
    } else {
        // Prepare and bind statement to prevent SQL injection
        $stmt = $conn->prepare("INSERT INTO users (name, email) VALUES (?, ?)");
        $stmt->bind_param("ss", $name, $email);

        // Execute and check success
        if ($stmt->execute()) {
            echo "New user record created successfully";
        } else {
            echo "Error: " . $stmt->error;
        }

        $stmt->close();
    }
} else {
    echo "Invalid request.";
}

$conn->close();
?>
```

In this example:

- We connect to the MySQL database and check the connection.
- We retrieve, sanitize, and validate user input.
- Prepared statements with bound parameters (bind_param()) help protect against SQL injection by treating input data as literal values.
- The script inserts the data into the users table if the data is valid.

Redirecting After Form Submission

It's common to redirect users after they submit a form to avoid duplicate submissions when they refresh the page. Use PHP's header() function to redirect.

php

```
header("Location: thank_you.php");
exit;
```

Place this code after the data is successfully processed to send users to a confirmation page.

In this chapter, we covered how to create forms, handle GET and POST requests, validate and sanitize input, and store form data in a MySQL database. Understanding these concepts is essential for developing interactive applications that process user input securely. In the next chapter, we'll explore PHP sessions and cookies, which allow for maintaining user information across different pages, essential for building features like user login systems.

CHAPTER 8: PHP SESSIONS AND COOKIES

Understanding Sessions and Cookies

Before diving into code, let's briefly discuss what sessions and cookies are and how they differ.

- **Sessions**: A session stores data on the server side and is uniquely identified by a session ID. When a user visits a website, PHP assigns them a unique session ID and stores it in a cookie or passes it in the URL. Sessions are ideal for storing sensitive information, such as login credentials, as they're more secure than cookies.

- **Cookies**: Cookies are small files stored on the client's browser, containing data that persists across multiple browsing sessions. They are often used to store less sensitive information, such as user preferences or settings. Cookies are visible to the client, so sensitive data should not be stored in them.

Using PHP Sessions

Sessions in PHP are easy to set up and use. They are helpful for applications requiring temporary data storage across pages, such as shopping carts or user authentication.

Starting a Session

To use sessions, you must first start the session with session_start() at the beginning of the PHP script. This function creates or resumes an existing session.

php

```php
<?php
session_start(); // Start or resume the session
```

Once the session is started, you can store data in the $_SESSION superglobal array.

Example: Creating a Login System with Sessions

Let's create a simple login system where users log in, and their status is remembered across pages.

1. **HTML Login Form**:

    html

    ```html
    <!DOCTYPE html>
    <html lang="en">
    <head>
        <meta charset="UTF-8">
    ```

```
    <title>Login</title>
</head>
<body>
  <h2>Login</h2>
  <form action="login.php" method="POST">
    <label for="username">Username:</label>
    <input type="text" id="username" name="username"
required>
    <label for="password">Password:</label>
    <input        type="password"        id="password"
name="password" required>
    <button type="submit">Login</button>
  </form>
</body>
</html>
```

2. **PHP Code to Process Login (login.php)**:

php

```php
<?php
session_start();

// Dummy user credentials for demonstration
$valid_username = "user";
$valid_password = "pass123";
```

```php
if ($_SERVER["REQUEST_METHOD"] == "POST") {
    $username = $_POST['username'];
    $password = $_POST['password'];

    // Check credentials
    if ($username === $valid_username && $password ===
$valid_password) {
        // Store user information in session
        $_SESSION['username'] = $username;
        $_SESSION['logged_in'] = true;
        header("Location: dashboard.php");
        exit;
    } else {
        echo "Invalid username or password.";
    }
}
?>
```

3. **Protected Page (dashboard.php)**:

php

```php
<?php
session_start();
```

```php
// Check if the user is logged in
if              (!isset($_SESSION['logged_in'])              ||
$_SESSION['logged_in'] !== true) {
   header("Location: login.php");
   exit;
}
?>


<!DOCTYPE html>
<html lang="en">
<head>
   <meta charset="UTF-8">
   <title>Dashboard</title>
</head>
<body>
   <h2>Welcome,                <?php                echo
htmlspecialchars($_SESSION['username']); ?>!</h2>
   <p>You are now logged in.</p>
   <a href="logout.php">Logout</a>
</body>
</html>
```

4. **Logging Out (logout.php)**:

php

```php
<?php
session_start();

// Destroy session data
session_unset();
session_destroy();

header("Location: login.php");
exit;
?>
```

Explanation:

- **Session Start**: Every page that relies on session data must start with session_start().
- **Setting Session Variables**: In login.php, when the user's credentials are verified, we set $_SESSION['username'] and $_SESSION['logged_in'] to true.
- **Access Control**: dashboard.php checks if $_SESSION['logged_in'] is set and true. If not, it redirects the user back to login.php.
- **Session Destruction**: logout.php clears all session data and destroys the session, logging the user out.

With this system, the user's login status is remembered across pages as long as the session is active.

Using PHP Cookies

Cookies store data on the client side and are often used to remember preferences or store small amounts of information across visits. Cookies are set using the setcookie() function and can be accessed through the $_COOKIE superglobal.

Creating a Cookie

The setcookie() function allows you to create a cookie. Here's the syntax:

php

setcookie(name, value, expire, path, domain, secure, httponly);
The essential parameters are:

- **name**: The name of the cookie.
- **value**: The value of the cookie.
- **expire**: The expiration time (in seconds), after which the cookie will be deleted. Use time() + seconds to set a future expiration.

Example: Setting a cookie to remember the user's preferred language for 30 days.

php

<?php

```
$language = "English";
setcookie("preferred_language", $language, time() + (30 * 24 * 60
* 60), "/"); // 30 days
```

This code creates a cookie named preferred_language with a value of "English" that expires in 30 days.

Retrieving a Cookie

You can access cookie data using the $_COOKIE superglobal array.

php

```
<?php
if (isset($_COOKIE["preferred_language"])) {
    echo "Preferred Language: " .
htmlspecialchars($_COOKIE["preferred_language"]);
} else {
    echo "No preferred language set.";
}
?>
```

Example: Personalizing Content with Cookies

Let's create an example where the user selects a theme for the website (dark or light mode), and we store their preference in a cookie.

1. **HTML Form to Select Theme**:

html

```
<!DOCTYPE html>
<html lang="en">
<head>
  <meta charset="UTF-8">
  <title>Select Theme</title>
</head>
<body>
  <h2>Select Your Theme</h2>
  <form action="set_theme.php" method="POST">
    <label>
      <input type="radio" name="theme" value="light" required> Light
    </label>
    <label>
      <input type="radio" name="theme" value="dark"> Dark
    </label>
    <button type="submit">Save Preference</button>
  </form>
</body>
</html>
```

2. **PHP Script to Set Theme Cookie (set_theme.php)**:

php

```php
<?php
if ($_SERVER["REQUEST_METHOD"] == "POST" &&
isset($_POST['theme'])) {
    $theme = $_POST['theme'];
    setcookie("theme", $theme, time() + (30 * 24 * 60 * 60),
"/"); // Set for 30 days
    header("Location: personalized_page.php");
    exit;
}
?>
```

3. **PHP Script to Apply Theme (personalized_page.php):**

php

```php
<?php
$theme = isset($_COOKIE['theme']) ? $_COOKIE['theme']
: 'light';
?>

<!DOCTYPE html>
<html lang="en">
<head>
    <meta charset="UTF-8">
```

```
<title>Personalized Page</title>
<style>
  body {
    background-color: <?php echo $theme === 'dark' ?
'#333' : '#fff'; ?>;
    color: <?php echo $theme === 'dark' ? '#fff' : '#000';
?>;
  }
</style>
</head>
<body>
  <h2>Welcome to Your <?php echo ucfirst($theme); ?>
Theme</h2>
  <p>Your theme preference has been saved and applied
to this page.</p>
  <a href="select_theme.php">Change Theme</a>
</body>
</html>
```

Explanation:

- **Theme Selection**: The user selects either "light" or "dark" mode in the HTML form, which is then submitted to set_theme.php.

- **Setting the Cookie**: set_theme.php stores the selected theme in a cookie named theme that expires in 30 days.

- **Applying the Theme**: personalized_page.php retrieves the theme from the $_COOKIE superglobal and applies it to the page using inline CSS.

This example shows how cookies can personalize content based on user preferences that persist across multiple visits.

Security Considerations

1. **Session Hijacking**: Session hijacking occurs when an attacker gains access to a user's session ID. To mitigate this risk:
   - Use session_regenerate_id() after login to create a new session ID.
   - Implement HTTPS to encrypt session data.
2. **Cookie Security**:
   - Use the httponly and secure flags in setcookie() to make cookies more secure.
   - Avoid storing sensitive information in cookies, as they are visible to the client.

In this chapter, you learned how to use sessions and cookies in PHP to manage user data across pages. Sessions are ideal for storing sensitive information on the server, while cookies store less sensitive data on the client's browser, allowing for a personalized experience across visits. With this knowledge, you can create login systems, remember user preferences, and maintain user states, enhancing the interactivity and personalization of your applications. In the next chapter, we'll dive into object-oriented PHP, which provides a more organized approach to structuring your code for larger projects.

CHAPTER 9: OBJECT-ORIENTED PHP

What is Object-Oriented Programming (OOP)?

Object-Oriented Programming (OOP) is a programming approach that organizes code around objects, which can represent real-world entities. Each object contains data (properties) and functions (methods) that act on that data. OOP aims to group related functionalities, making it easier to model complex systems, reuse code, and reduce duplication.

Key Concepts in OOP:

- **Classes**: Templates for creating objects. A class defines the properties and methods that the object will have.
- **Objects**: Instances of classes. When you create an object, you instantiate a class, allowing you to interact with its properties and methods.
- **Properties**: Variables within a class that hold data specific to each object.

- **Methods**: Functions defined within a class that perform operations on the properties.

Advantages of OOP in PHP

Using OOP in PHP has several benefits:

1. **Code Reusability**: Classes can be reused across projects, reducing redundancy.
2. **Modularity**: Code is organized into self-contained classes, making it easier to maintain and debug.
3. **Extensibility**: OOP principles like inheritance allow classes to extend each other, adding new functionality while reusing existing code.
4. **Abstraction**: Complex systems can be broken down into simpler, more manageable parts, improving readability and organization.

Basic Concepts of OOP in PHP

Let's start with the fundamental OOP concepts in PHP, focusing on classes, objects, properties, and methods.

Defining a Class

A class in PHP is defined using the class keyword, followed by the class name and curly braces containing the properties and methods.

php

```php
<?php
class Car {
    // Properties
    public $make;
    public $model;
    public $year;

    // Method to set car details
    public function setDetails($make, $model, $year) {
        $this->make = $make;
        $this->model = $model;
        $this->year = $year;
    }

    // Method to get car details
    public function getDetails() {
        return "$this->year $this->make $this->model";
    }
}
?>
```

In this example:

- **Class Definition**: Car is a class representing a car.
- **Properties**: $make, $model, and $year are properties of the Car class.

- **Methods**: setDetails() sets the car details, and getDetails() returns a formatted string of those details.
- **$this Keyword**: Refers to the current object instance, allowing access to properties and methods within the class.

Creating an Object

Once you have defined a class, you can create an object (an instance of that class) and interact with its properties and methods.

php

```php
<?php
// Create an instance of the Car class
$myCar = new Car();

// Set car details
$myCar->setDetails("Toyota", "Camry", 2022);

// Get and display car details
echo $myCar->getDetails();  // Outputs: 2022 Toyota Camry
?>
```

Explanation:

- **Instantiation**: $myCar = new Car(); creates a new Car object.

- **Method Calls**: $myCar->setDetails() sets the car properties, and $myCar->getDetails() retrieves them.

Access Modifiers

Access modifiers define the visibility of class properties and methods. PHP has three main access modifiers:

1. **Public**: Accessible from anywhere. This is the default visibility.
2. **Protected**: Accessible only within the class itself and by inheriting subclasses.
3. **Private**: Accessible only within the class that defines it, not by subclasses or from outside the class.

php

```php
<?php
class Person {
    public $name;       // Public property
    protected $age;     // Protected property
    private $salary;    // Private property

    public function setSalary($amount) {
        $this->salary = $amount;
    }
```

```php
    public function getSalary() {
        return $this->salary;
    }
}
?>
```

In this example:

- $name is a public property and can be accessed from outside the class.
- $age is protected and can only be accessed within the Person class or its subclasses.
- $salary is private and can only be accessed by methods within the Person class, such as setSalary() and getSalary().

Constructors and Destructors

- **Constructor**: A special method automatically called when an object is created. Constructors are often used to initialize properties.
- **Destructor**: A method called when an object is destroyed, typically used for cleanup tasks.

In PHP, constructors and destructors are defined using __construct and __destruct.

php

```php
<?php
class User {
    public $username;

    // Constructor
    public function __construct($username) {
        $this->username = $username;
        echo "User $username created.<br>";
    }

    // Destructor
    public function __destruct() {
        echo "User $this->username destroyed.<br>";
    }
}

// Create a User object
$user = new User("john_doe");
?>
```

In this example:

- __construct() is called immediately after creating the User object, outputting "User john_doe created."
- __destruct() is called when the script ends or the object is explicitly destroyed, outputting "User john_doe destroyed."

Inheritance

Inheritance allows a class to inherit properties and methods from another class. In PHP, a class can inherit from only one class (single inheritance) using the extends keyword.

php

```php
<?php
class Animal {
    public $name;

    public function speak() {
        echo "$this->name makes a sound.<br>";
    }
}


class Dog extends Animal {
    public function speak() {
        echo "$this->name barks.<br>";
    }
}


// Create instances
$animal = new Animal();
$animal->name = "Animal";
$animal->speak();  // Outputs: Animal makes a sound.
```

```php
$dog = new Dog();
$dog->name = "Buddy";
$dog->speak();    // Outputs: Buddy barks.
?>
```

In this example:

- Animal is the base class with a speak() method.
- Dog extends Animal and overrides the speak() method to provide a specialized behavior.

Polymorphism

Polymorphism allows classes to be used interchangeably because they share a common interface or base class. PHP supports polymorphism through **method overriding** and **interfaces**.

Method Overriding

A subclass can override a method inherited from the parent class. We saw this in the Dog class, which overrides the speak() method of the Animal class.

Interfaces

An interface defines a set of methods that implementing classes must provide. Interfaces are used to ensure a consistent method structure across different classes.

php

```php
<?php
interface Payable {
    public function calculatePay();
}

class Employee implements Payable {
    public function calculatePay() {
        return 2000;
    }
}

class Contractor implements Payable {
    public function calculatePay() {
        return 1500;
    }
}

$employee = new Employee();
$contractor = new Contractor();
echo $employee->calculatePay();    // Outputs: 2000
echo $contractor->calculatePay();  // Outputs: 1500
?>
```

In this example:

- Payable is an interface with a calculatePay() method.

- Employee and Contractor both implement Payable and provide their own implementations of calculatePay().

Encapsulation

Encapsulation is an OOP principle that restricts direct access to some of an object's properties and methods. Instead, data is accessed through public methods. This protects data integrity and keeps the internal workings of a class hidden from the outside.

php

```php
<?php
class BankAccount {
    private $balance = 0;

    public function deposit($amount) {
        if ($amount > 0) {
            $this->balance += $amount;
        }
    }

    public function getBalance() {
        return $this->balance;
    }
}
```

```php
$account = new BankAccount();
$account->deposit(500);
echo $account->getBalance();  // Outputs: 500
?>
```

In this example:

- $balance is a private property, ensuring it cannot be accessed directly.
- deposit() and getBalance() are public methods, providing controlled access to $balance.

Creating a Real-World Example: Product Catalog

Let's put these concepts together by creating a simple product catalog system with a base Product class and a specialized Electronics class.

1. **Define the Base Class**:

   php

```php
<?php
class Product {
    protected $name;
    protected $price;

    public function __construct($name, $price) {
        $this->name = $name;
```

```php
        $this->price = $price;
    }


    public function display() {
        return "Product: $this->name, Price: $$this->price";
    }
}
?>
```

2. **Define a Subclass**:

php

```php
<?php
class Electronics extends Product {
    private $warranty;


    public function __construct($name, $price, $warranty) {
        parent::__construct($name, $price);
        $this->warranty = $warranty;
    }


    public function display() {
        return parent::display() . ", Warranty: $this->warranty
years";
    }
```

```
}
?>
```

3. **Instantiate and Use the Classes**:

php

```php
<?php
$phone = new Electronics("Smartphone", 699, 2);
echo $phone->display();  // Outputs: Product: Smartphone,
Price: $699, Warranty: 2 years
?>
```

In this example:

- Product is a base class with properties for name and price.
- Electronics extends Product and adds a warranty property.
- The display() method in Electronics overrides the base class's method to include warranty details.

In this chapter, we introduced object-oriented programming (OOP) in PHP, covering the core concepts of classes, objects, inheritance, polymorphism, encapsulation, and interfaces. OOP allows for cleaner, more modular, and more maintainable code, making it a valuable tool as applications grow in size and complexity. In the next chapter, we'll explore CRUD operations in PHP and MySQL, using OOP principles to manage and organize data more effectively.

CHAPTER 10: CRUD OPERATIONS WITH PHP AND MYSQL

Setting Up the Database

Let's start by setting up a sample MySQL database and table for this chapter. We'll create a database named library and a table called books, which will store information about books, including title, author, and publication year.

1. **Creating the Database**:

   sql

   CREATE DATABASE library;

2. **Creating the Table**:

   sql

   USE library;

```
CREATE TABLE books (
    id INT AUTO_INCREMENT PRIMARY KEY,
    title VARCHAR(255) NOT NULL,
    author VARCHAR(255) NOT NULL,
    year INT NOT NULL
);
```

The books table has four columns:

- id: A unique identifier for each book (primary key).
- title: The title of the book.
- author: The author of the book.
- year: The publication year.

Connecting PHP to the Database

Before performing CRUD operations, we need to establish a connection to the database. Here's a reusable connection script.

php

```php
<?php
// Database connection settings
$servername = "localhost";
$username = "root";
$password = "";
$dbname = "library";
```

```php
// Create connection
$conn = new mysqli($servername, $username, $password, $dbname);

// Check connection
if ($conn->connect_error) {
    die("Connection failed: " . $conn->connect_error);
}
?>
```

This script connects to the library database using the MySQLi extension. If the connection fails, it outputs an error message.

Create Operation

The **Create** operation adds new records to the books table. We'll create a form where users can input book details and save them to the database.

1. **HTML Form for Adding a Book**:

   html

```html
<!DOCTYPE html>
<html lang="en">
<head>
    <meta charset="UTF-8">
```

```html
    <title>Add Book</title>
</head>
<body>
    <h2>Add a New Book</h2>
    <form action="add_book.php" method="POST">
        <label for="title">Title:</label>
        <input type="text" id="title" name="title" required>
        <label for="author">Author:</label>
        <input type="text" id="author" name="author" required>
        <label for="year">Publication Year:</label>
        <input type="number" id="year" name="year" required>
        <button type="submit">Add Book</button>
    </form>
</body>
</html>
```

2. **PHP Code to Handle Form Submission (add_book.php)**:

php

```php
<?php
include 'db_connection.php'; // Include the database connection
```

```php
if ($_SERVER["REQUEST_METHOD"] == "POST") {
    // Retrieve and sanitize form data
    $title = htmlspecialchars($_POST['title']);
    $author = htmlspecialchars($_POST['author']);
    $year = (int)$_POST['year'];

    // Prepare and execute the insert query
    $stmt = $conn->prepare("INSERT INTO books (title, author, year) VALUES (?, ?, ?)");
    $stmt->bind_param("ssi", $title, $author, $year);

    if ($stmt->execute()) {
        echo "New book added successfully.";
    } else {
        echo "Error: " . $stmt->error;
    }

    $stmt->close();
}

$conn->close();
?>
```

Explanation:

- We retrieve form data using $_POST, sanitize it using htmlspecialchars(), and bind it to the SQL query.

- bind_param("ssi", $title, $author, $year) binds the parameters, where "ssi" represents the data types (string, string, integer).

Read Operation

The **Read** operation retrieves and displays records from the books table. This is useful for displaying a list of books on a web page.

PHP Code to Display All Books (view_books.php):

php

```php
<?php
include 'db_connection.php'; // Include the database connection

$sql = "SELECT id, title, author, year FROM books";
$result = $conn->query($sql);
?>
```

```html
<!DOCTYPE html>
<html lang="en">
<head>
  <meta charset="UTF-8">
  <title>Book List</title>
</head>
<body>
  <h2>Book List</h2>
```

```php
<table border="1">
  <tr>
    <th>ID</th>
    <th>Title</th>
    <th>Author</th>
    <th>Year</th>
    <th>Actions</th>
  </tr>
  <?php
  if ($result->num_rows > 0) {
      while ($row = $result->fetch_assoc()) {
          echo "<tr>";
          echo "<td>" . htmlspecialchars($row["id"]) . "</td>";
          echo "<td>" . htmlspecialchars($row["title"]) . "</td>";
          echo "<td>" . htmlspecialchars($row["author"]) . "</td>";
          echo "<td>" . htmlspecialchars($row["year"]) . "</td>";
          echo "<td><a href='edit_book.php?id=" . $row["id"] . "'>Edit</a> | <a href='delete_book.php?id=" . $row["id"] . "'>Delete</a></td>";
          echo "</tr>";
      }
  } else {
      echo "<tr><td colspan='5'>No books found.</td></tr>";
  }
```

```
    ?>
  </table>
</body>
</html>
```

```php
<?php
$conn->close();
?>
```

Explanation:

- We query the books table for all records and loop through the results, displaying each row in a table.
- Each row includes "Edit" and "Delete" links for managing individual records.

Update Operation

The **Update** operation allows users to modify existing records. We'll add an "Edit" form where users can update book details.

1. **PHP Code to Display the Edit Form (edit_book.php)**:

   php

```php
<?php
include 'db_connection.php';

// Check if an ID was provided in the URL
```

```php
if (isset($_GET['id'])) {
    $id = (int)$_GET['id'];
    $sql = "SELECT * FROM books WHERE id = ?";
    $stmt = $conn->prepare($sql);
    $stmt->bind_param("i", $id);
    $stmt->execute();
    $result = $stmt->get_result();
    $book = $result->fetch_assoc();
    $stmt->close();
} else {
    echo "No book ID specified.";
    exit;
}
?>


<!DOCTYPE html>
<html lang="en">
<head>
    <meta charset="UTF-8">
    <title>Edit Book</title>
</head>
<body>
    <h2>Edit Book</h2>
    <form action="update_book.php" method="POST">
```

```
<input type="hidden" name="id" value="<?php echo
htmlspecialchars($book['id']); ?>">
<label for="title">Title:</label>
<input type="text" id="title" name="title"
value="<?php echo htmlspecialchars($book['title']); ?>"
required>
<label for="author">Author:</label>
<input type="text" id="author" name="author"
value="<?php echo htmlspecialchars($book['author']); ?>"
required>
<label for="year">Publication Year:</label>
<input type="number" id="year" name="year"
value="<?php echo htmlspecialchars($book['year']); ?>"
required>
<button type="submit">Update Book</button>
</form>
</body>
</html>
```

2. **PHP Code to Update the Record (update_book.php)**:

php

```
<?php
include 'db_connection.php';
```

```php
if ($_SERVER["REQUEST_METHOD"] == "POST") {
    $id = (int)$_POST['id'];
    $title = htmlspecialchars($_POST['title']);
    $author = htmlspecialchars($_POST['author']);
    $year = (int)$_POST['year'];

    $stmt = $conn->prepare("UPDATE books SET title = ?,
author = ?, year = ? WHERE id = ?");
    $stmt->bind_param("ssii", $title, $author, $year, $id);

    if ($stmt->execute()) {
        echo "Book updated successfully.";
    } else {
        echo "Error: " . $stmt->error;
    }

    $stmt->close();
}

$conn->close();
?>
```

Explanation:

- edit_book.php retrieves the existing data for the selected book, displaying it in a form for editing.

- update_book.php processes the form, updating the record in the database based on the book ID.

Delete Operation

The **Delete** operation removes a record from the books table.

PHP Code to Delete a Book (delete_book.php):

php

```php
<?php
include 'db_connection.php';

if (isset($_GET['id'])) {
    $id = (int)$_GET['id'];
    $stmt = $conn->prepare("DELETE FROM books WHERE id = ?");
    $stmt->bind_param("i", $id);

    if ($stmt->execute()) {
        echo "Book deleted successfully.";
    } else {
        echo "Error: " . $stmt->error;
    }

    $stmt->close();
}
```

```
$conn->close();
?>
```

Explanation:

- This script retrieves the book ID from the URL and deletes the corresponding record from the books table.

In this chapter, you learned how to perform CRUD operations in PHP with MySQL, creating, reading, updating, and deleting records in a books table. These operations are fundamental for any database-driven application and allow you to build dynamic, data-centric features. In the next chapter, we'll dive into error handling and debugging in PHP and MySQL, so you can troubleshoot issues effectively and ensure the reliability of your application.

CHAPTER 11: ERROR HANDLING AND DEBUGGING

Types of Errors in PHP

In PHP, there are several types of errors that developers commonly encounter:

1. **Syntax Errors**: Occur when PHP code is malformed, such as missing a semicolon or unmatched parentheses. These prevent scripts from running at all.

2. **Runtime Errors**: Occur while the script is running, such as trying to divide by zero or access a nonexistent file.

3. **Logical Errors**: Mistakes in the logic of the code, often leading to unexpected results (e.g., incorrect calculations or unintended output).

4. **Database Errors**: Errors that occur when interacting with MySQL, such as syntax issues in SQL queries, connection issues, or attempting to operate on non-existent tables.

By implementing error handling and debugging practices, you can catch and address these issues more effectively.

Configuring PHP Error Reporting

To aid debugging, you can configure PHP to display or log errors. PHP's error_reporting function allows you to control which errors are reported.

1. **Display Errors During Development**: In a development environment, displaying errors helps identify issues quickly. In your php.ini file or at the start of your script, enable error reporting:

    php

    ```
    ini_set('display_errors', 1);
    ini_set('display_startup_errors', 1);
    error_reporting(E_ALL);
    ```

2. **Hide Errors in Production**: In a production environment, you generally want to hide errors to avoid exposing sensitive information. Instead, log errors to a file.

    php

    ```
    ini_set('display_errors', 0);
    ini_set('log_errors', 1);
    ini_set('error_log', '/path/to/php-error.log');
    error_reporting(E_ALL);
    ```

Explanation:

- display_errors: Determines whether errors are shown in the browser.
- log_errors: Enables error logging.
- error_log: Specifies the file where errors are logged.
- error_reporting(E_ALL): Reports all errors, warnings, and notices.

Basic Error Handling in PHP

PHP offers several built-in error-handling functions and structures that allow you to manage errors and exceptions effectively.

Try-Catch Blocks

In PHP, exceptions are used to handle unexpected events gracefully. The try-catch block lets you "try" a piece of code and "catch" any exceptions that occur, allowing for custom error handling.

php

```php
<?php
try {
    $conn = new mysqli("localhost", "invalid_user", "invalid_password", "library");
    if ($conn->connect_error) {
        throw new Exception("Connection failed: " . $conn->connect_error);
    }
```

```php
    echo "Connected successfully";
} catch (Exception $e) {
    echo "Error: " . $e->getMessage();
}
?>
```

Explanation:

- If the connection fails, throw new Exception() triggers an exception.
- catch (Exception $e) catches the exception and outputs a custom error message.

This method provides better control over error handling, allowing you to log, display, or handle errors as needed.

Handling Database Errors

When interacting with MySQL, it's important to handle potential errors from database operations.

Example: Error handling with prepared statements

php

```php
<?php
include 'db_connection.php';

try {
```

```php
$stmt = $conn->prepare("INSERT INTO books (title, author, year) VALUES (?, ?, ?)");
    if (!$stmt) {
        throw new Exception("Failed to prepare statement: " . $conn->error);
    }

    $title = "1984";
    $author = "George Orwell";
    $year = 1949;
    $stmt->bind_param("ssi", $title, $author, $year);

    if (!$stmt->execute()) {
        throw new Exception("Execution failed: " . $stmt->error);
    }

    echo "Book added successfully.";
    $stmt->close();
} catch (Exception $e) {
    echo "Error: " . $e->getMessage();
    error_log($e->getMessage(), 3, "/path/to/db-error.log"); // Log error to file
}

$conn->close();
```

```
?>
```

In this example:

- We use throw new Exception() to handle errors with prepared statements.
- error_log($e->getMessage(), 3, "/path/to/db-error.log"); logs the error to a custom file for future review.

Custom Error Handling

PHP allows you to create a custom error handler function using set_error_handler(). This function can define specific actions to take when an error occurs, such as logging the error or sending an alert.

Example: Custom error handler

php

```php
<?php
function customErrorHandler($errno, $errstr, $errfile, $errline) {
    $errorMessage = "[Error $errno] $errstr in $errfile on line $errline";
    echo "Oops! Something went wrong. Please try again later.";
    error_log($errorMessage, 3, "/path/to/custom-error.log"); // Log error to file
}
// Set custom error handler
```

```php
set_error_handler("customErrorHandler");

// Trigger an error for demonstration
echo $undefinedVariable;
?>
```

Explanation:

- customErrorHandler() is triggered whenever an error occurs. It displays a generic message to the user and logs the details to a file.
- set_error_handler("customErrorHandler") sets this function as the active error handler.

This method is helpful for handling errors more flexibly and securely, as you can define actions based on the error type.

Debugging Techniques

Here are some essential debugging techniques and tools for PHP and MySQL applications.

Using var_dump and print_r

var_dump and print_r are invaluable tools for displaying variable values, helping you understand the state of your application at various points.

php

```php
<?php
$data = array("title" => "To Kill a Mockingbird", "author" =>
"Harper Lee");
var_dump($data); // Displays detailed information about the
variable
print_r($data); // Displays readable information about the variable
?>
```

Both functions print variable contents, but var_dump shows more detailed information, such as data types and lengths.

PHP Error Log

Reviewing error logs is essential for tracking and troubleshooting issues, especially in production. The PHP error log (/path/to/php-error.log) can reveal details about failed database connections, undefined variables, and other runtime issues.

Example of reading the last 10 lines of an error log (Linux command):

bash

```bash
tail -n 10 /path/to/php-error.log
```

MySQL Error Log

Similarly, MySQL maintains its own error log, where you can find details about failed queries, connection issues, and other database-related errors.

For example, MySQL logs can be found in default locations like /var/log/mysql/error.log on Linux. Use tail to view recent entries:

bash

tail -n 10 /var/log/mysql/error.log

Testing SQL Queries

Often, errors in MySQL operations arise from incorrect SQL syntax or logic. Testing SQL queries directly in phpMyAdmin or the MySQL command line can help you identify and fix issues before incorporating them into PHP code.

1. **Run the Query in phpMyAdmin**: Paste the SQL query into phpMyAdmin's SQL tab and execute it. This provides immediate feedback on whether the query works.

2. **Check for Common Errors**:
   o Missing or extra commas and parentheses.
   o Misspelled table or column names.
   o Incorrect data types (e.g., trying to insert a string into an integer column).

Using debug_backtrace for Tracing

PHP's debug_backtrace() function provides a trace of the function calls leading to a particular point in your code. This can be invaluable for understanding the sequence of events in complex applications.

Example:

php

```php
<?php
function testFunction() {
    anotherFunction();
}

function anotherFunction() {
    thirdFunction();
}

function thirdFunction() {
    debug_print_backtrace();
}

testFunction();
?>
```

The output shows the chain of function calls, helping you track how and where a particular error occurred.

Practical Troubleshooting Tips

Here are some troubleshooting tips for common issues encountered in PHP and MySQL development.

1. **Database Connection Issues**:

- o Ensure the database server is running.
- o Check your database credentials (username, password, hostname).
- o Use error handling with connection code to display or log specific issues.

2. **Undefined Variable Notices**:
   - o Initialize all variables to avoid undefined notices.
   - o Use isset() to check if variables are set before accessing them.

3. **Query Syntax Errors**:
   - o Copy the query and test it directly in phpMyAdmin to identify syntax issues.
   - o Ensure that values are properly escaped or use prepared statements to avoid SQL injection.

4. **Session Issues**:
   - o Always call session_start() at the beginning of any script that relies on session data.
   - o Use print_r($_SESSION) to inspect session contents if session data appears incorrect.

In this chapter, you learned how to manage and log errors in PHP and MySQL, including using error reporting, try-catch blocks, custom error handling, and practical debugging techniques. With these skills, you can troubleshoot issues effectively and maintain a more stable application, providing a better experience for your users. In the next chapter, we'll discuss working with files in PHP, covering file upload, read, write, and manipulation tasks.

CHAPTER 12: WORKING WITH FILES IN PHP

File Uploading in PHP

PHP provides built-in functionality to handle file uploads from an HTML form. When users upload a file, PHP temporarily stores it on the server and provides access through the $_FILES superglobal array.

Step 1: Creating an HTML Form for File Upload

Let's start by creating a form where users can upload a file. The form's enctype attribute must be set to "multipart/form-data" for file uploads.

html

```
<!DOCTYPE html>
<html lang="en">
<head>
   <meta charset="UTF-8">
   <title>Upload File</title>
</head>
<body>
   <h2>Upload a File</h2>
   <form          action="upload.php"          method="POST"
enctype="multipart/form-data">
```

```
    <label for="file">Choose a file:</label>
    <input type="file" id="file" name="file" required>
    <button type="submit">Upload</button>
  </form>
</body>
</html>
```

Explanation:

- **<input type="file">**: Allows users to select a file from their device.

- **enctype="multipart/form-data"**: Specifies that the form will contain file data, ensuring it's sent correctly.

Step 2: PHP Code to Process the File Upload (upload.php)

In the PHP script, we handle the file upload by accessing information from $_FILES['file'], such as the file name, type, temporary location, and any errors.

php

```php
<?php
if ($_SERVER["REQUEST_METHOD"] == "POST") {
   // Define the directory where files will be uploaded
   $uploadDirectory = "uploads/";

   // Access file details from $_FILES array
```

```php
$fileName = basename($_FILES["file"]["name"]);
$fileTmpName = $_FILES["file"]["tmp_name"];
$fileSize = $_FILES["file"]["size"];
$fileType = $_FILES["file"]["type"];
$fileError = $_FILES["file"]["error"];

// Define the target path
$targetFilePath = $uploadDirectory . $fileName;

// Check for upload errors
if ($fileError === UPLOAD_ERR_OK) {
    // Validate file type (e.g., allow only images)
    $allowedTypes = ["image/jpeg", "image/png", "image/gif"];
    if (in_array($fileType, $allowedTypes)) {
        // Move file to the upload directory
        if (move_uploaded_file($fileTmpName, $targetFilePath)) {
            echo    "File    uploaded    successfully:    "    .
htmlspecialchars($fileName);
        } else {
            echo "Error uploading the file.";
        }
    } else {
        echo "Invalid file type. Only JPG, PNG, and GIF files are
allowed.";
    }
```

```
   } else {
      echo "Error: " . $fileError;
   }
}
?>
```

Explanation:

- **$uploadDirectory**: Directory where files will be stored (must exist and be writable).
- **File Validation**: Checks file type to allow only specific formats (e.g., images).
- **move_uploaded_file()**: Moves the file from the temporary directory to the specified location.

File Upload Security Considerations

When handling file uploads, it's essential to validate the file and ensure it's stored securely to prevent attacks.

- **File Type Validation**: Check the file's MIME type (e.g., only allow image types).
- **File Size Limit**: Set a maximum file size to prevent large uploads that could slow down or crash your server.
- **Unique Filenames**: Generate unique names for uploaded files to avoid overwriting and for added security (e.g., use uniqid() or hash the file name).

- **Restrict File Access**: Store uploaded files outside the public root if sensitive and use scripts to access them.

Reading and Writing Files in PHP

PHP provides several functions for reading from and writing to files, making it easy to manage files on the server.

Opening and Closing Files

To read or write to a file, you need to open it with fopen(), specifying the mode:

- **"r"**: Read-only
- **"w"**: Write-only (truncates the file or creates a new one)
- **"a"**: Append (writes data at the end)
- **"x"**: Create new (fails if the file already exists)

Example: Opening and closing a file

php

```php
<?php
$filename = "example.txt";
$file = fopen($filename, "r"); // Open for reading

if ($file) {
    echo "File opened successfully.<br>";
    fclose($file); // Close the file
```

```php
} else {
    echo "Failed to open the file.";
}
?>
```

Reading a File

PHP provides several functions to read files, including fread(), fgets(), and file_get_contents().

1. **Reading the Entire File with file_get_contents():**

   php

   ```php
   <?php
   $filename = "example.txt";
   $content = file_get_contents($filename);
   if ($content !== false) {
       echo nl2br(htmlspecialchars($content));
   } else {
       echo "Failed to read the file.";
   }
   ?>
   ```

2. **Reading Line by Line with fgets():**

   php

```php
<?php
$filename = "example.txt";
$file = fopen($filename, "r");

if ($file) {
    while (($line = fgets($file)) !== false) {
        echo htmlspecialchars($line) . "<br>";
    }
    fclose($file);
} else {
    echo "Failed to open the file.";
}
?>
```

Explanation:

- **file_get_contents()** reads the entire file into a string, ideal for small files.
- **fgets()** reads one line at a time, which is useful for larger files or line-by-line processing.

Writing to a File

Writing data to a file is similar to reading but requires an appropriate mode, such as "w" or "a".

Example: Writing data to a file

php

```php
<?php
$filename = "example.txt";
$data = "Hello, world!";

$file = fopen($filename, "w");
if ($file) {
    fwrite($file, $data);
    fclose($file);
    echo "Data written successfully.";
} else {
    echo "Failed to open the file for writing.";
}
?>
```

Explanation:

- **fwrite()** writes data to the file. If opened in "w" mode, the file is overwritten; in "a" mode, data is appended.

File Management in PHP

PHP includes functions to manage files and directories, such as renaming, deleting, and checking file properties.

Renaming and Deleting Files

- **Renaming a File**: Use rename() to change a file's name or move it to another directory.

php

```php
<?php
if (rename("oldfile.txt", "newfile.txt")) {
    echo "File renamed successfully.";
} else {
    echo "Failed to rename the file.";
}
?>
```

- **Deleting a File**: Use unlink() to delete a file from the filesystem.

php

```php
<?php
if (unlink("file_to_delete.txt")) {
    echo "File deleted successfully.";
} else {
    echo "Failed to delete the file.";
}
?>
```

Checking File Existence and Properties

- **file_exists()**: Check if a file exists.

php

```php
<?php
if (file_exists("example.txt")) {
    echo "File exists.";
} else {
    echo "File does not exist.";
}
?>
```

- **filesize()**: Get the file size in bytes.

php

```php
<?php
echo "File size: " . filesize("example.txt") . " bytes";
?>
```

- **is_readable() and is_writable()**: Check if a file is readable or writable.

php

```php
<?php
if (is_readable("example.txt")) {
    echo "File is readable.";
}
```

```php
if (is_writable("example.txt")) {
    echo "File is writable.";
}
?>
```

Example: File Upload and Display

Let's combine file upload and file management by creating an application where users can upload images, and the application displays them in a gallery.

1. **HTML Form for Image Upload** (upload form from earlier).

2. **PHP Script to Handle Upload and Display Gallery** (upload_and_display.php):

php

```php
<?php
$uploadDirectory = "uploads/";

// Handle file upload
if ($_SERVER["REQUEST_METHOD"] == "POST" &&
isset($_FILES["file"])) {
    $fileName = basename($_FILES["file"]["name"]);
    $targetFilePath = $uploadDirectory . $fileName;
```

```php
    if (move_uploaded_file($_FILES["file"]["tmp_name"],
$targetFilePath)) {
        echo "File uploaded successfully: " .
htmlspecialchars($fileName);
    } else {
        echo "Error uploading file.";
    }
}


// Display uploaded images as a gallery
echo "<h2>Gallery</h2>";
$files = scandir($uploadDirectory);
foreach ($files as $file) {
    if ($file !== "." && $file !== "..") {
        echo "<img src='" . $uploadDirectory . $file . "' alt='" .
htmlspecialchars($file) . "' width='100'>";
    }
}
?>
```

Explanation:

- **File Upload**: Saves the uploaded file to the uploads/ directory.
- **Image Gallery**: Uses scandir() to list files in the uploads/ directory and display them as thumbnails.

In this chapter, we covered essential file-handling techniques in PHP, including file uploading, reading, writing, and managing files. Working with files opens up many possibilities for your applications, from image galleries to document management systems. In the next chapter, we'll explore the Model-View-Controller (MVC) architecture, which provides a structured approach to organizing and managing larger PHP applications.

CHAPTER 13: INTRODUCTION TO MVC ARCHITECTURE

What is MVC?

MVC stands for **Model-View-Controller**, a design pattern that organizes application code into three interconnected components:

1. **Model**: Manages data, business logic, and interactions with the database.
2. **View**: Handles the presentation layer, displaying data to the user in a specific format.
3. **Controller**: Acts as an intermediary between the Model and the View, handling user input, updating the Model, and determining which View to display.

Each component has a specific role:

- The **Model** is responsible for data handling and validation.
- The **View** focuses on presenting data to the user, using HTML and CSS for formatting.
- The **Controller** processes user requests and determines the appropriate responses.

This separation of responsibilities enables better organization, making it easier to maintain and scale your application as it grows.

How MVC Works: A Step-by-Step Example

Here's an overview of how MVC works in a typical web application workflow:

1. **User Request**: The user interacts with the application (e.g., by clicking a link or submitting a form). This sends a request to the server.

2. **Controller Handles Request**: The Controller receives the request and decides which action to take. It often retrieves or updates data via the Model.

3. **Model Manages Data**: The Model handles data operations, such as retrieving information from the database or validating input.

4. **Controller Updates View**: The Controller passes data from the Model to the View, which formats and displays it to the user.

5. **Response Displayed to User**: The View renders the response, and the user sees the final output in their browser.

By following this sequence, the MVC pattern ensures a clear division between the logic, data, and presentation layers.

Components of MVC in Detail

Let's dive deeper into each MVC component to understand its responsibilities and how it interacts with the other components.

1. Model

The Model represents the data and business logic of the application. It's responsible for:

- **Data Storage**: The Model interacts with the database, handling CRUD operations (Create, Read, Update, Delete).
- **Business Logic**: It enforces application rules and validations, ensuring data integrity.
- **Data Processing**: The Model prepares data for the Controller to pass to the View.

Example: A simple User Model that handles retrieving and saving user data.

php

```php
<?php
class User {
    private $conn;

    public function __construct($dbConnection) {
        $this->conn = $dbConnection;
    }

    public function getUserById($id) {
        $stmt = $this->conn->prepare("SELECT * FROM users WHERE id = ?");
```

```php
    $stmt->bind_param("i", $id);
    $stmt->execute();
    return $stmt->get_result()->fetch_assoc();
}


    public function createUser($name, $email) {
    $stmt = $this->conn->prepare("INSERT INTO users (name,
email) VALUES (?, ?)");
    $stmt->bind_param("ss", $name, $email);
    return $stmt->execute();
    }
}
?>
```

In this example:

- The User Model manages database interactions.
- getUserById() retrieves user data by ID, while createUser() inserts new user data.

2. View

The View is responsible for displaying the data to the user. It contains HTML, CSS, and sometimes minimal PHP to render dynamic content. The View should not contain complex business logic; its role is to present data in a user-friendly format.

Example: A View template for displaying a user's profile.

php

```
<!DOCTYPE html>
<html lang="en">
<head>
    <meta charset="UTF-8">
    <title>User Profile</title>
</head>
<body>
    <h1>User Profile</h1>
    <p>Name: <?php echo htmlspecialchars($user['name']); ?></p>
    <p>Email: <?php echo htmlspecialchars($user['email']); ?></p>
</body>
</html>
```

In this example:

- The View receives the $user data from the Controller and displays it with minimal PHP for output.
- The View's focus is on presentation, so it includes HTML structure and styling but avoids complex logic.

3. Controller

The Controller handles the flow of the application. It receives user input, interacts with the Model to retrieve or update data, and passes data to the View. The Controller orchestrates actions between the Model and View.

Example: A UserController class that handles displaying a user's profile.

php

```php
<?php
class UserController {
    private $model;

    public function __construct($userModel) {
        $this->model = $userModel;
    }

    public function showProfile($id) {
        // Retrieve data from the model
        $user = $this->model->getUserById($id);

        // Include the view and pass data
        include "views/user_profile.php";
    }
}
?>
```

In this example:

- The UserController interacts with the User Model to retrieve user data based on an ID.

- It then includes the appropriate View (user_profile.php) and passes the retrieved $user data for display.

Setting Up an MVC Application in PHP

To build an MVC application in PHP, we'll organize files and directories by their roles.

1. Directory Structure

Here's a typical MVC directory structure:

lua

```
/mvc-app
|-- /controllers
|   |-- UserController.php
|
|-- /models
|   |-- User.php
|
|-- /views
|   |-- user_profile.php
|
|-- /config
|   |-- database.php
|
```

|-- index.php

- **/controllers**: Stores Controller classes, each responsible for a specific part of the application.
- **/models**: Contains Model classes that handle data-related operations.
- **/views**: Holds View templates, responsible for presenting data to the user.
- **/config**: Contains configuration files, such as database connections.
- **index.php**: The entry point of the application, which routes user requests to the appropriate Controller.

2. Creating a Simple MVC Flow

Let's put together a complete MVC example using the User model and UserController from above.

1. **Database Configuration** (config/database.php):

php

```php
<?php
function getDatabaseConnection() {
    $servername = "localhost";
    $username = "root";
    $password = "";
    $dbname = "mvc_app";
```

```php
    $conn    =    new    mysqli($servername,    $username,
$password, $dbname);
    if ($conn->connect_error) {
        die("Connection failed: " . $conn->connect_error);
    }
    return $conn;
}
?>
```

2. **User Model** (models/User.php):

php

```php
<?php
class User {
    private $conn;

    public function __construct($dbConnection) {
        $this->conn = $dbConnection;
    }

    public function getUserById($id) {
        $stmt = $this->conn->prepare("SELECT * FROM
users WHERE id = ?");
        $stmt->bind_param("i", $id);
```

```php
    $stmt->execute();
    return $stmt->get_result()->fetch_assoc();
  }
}
?>
```

3. **User Controller** (controllers/UserController.php):

php

```php
<?php
class UserController {
    private $model;

    public function __construct($userModel) {
        $this->model = $userModel;
    }

    public function showProfile($id) {
        $user = $this->model->getUserById($id);
        include "views/user_profile.php";
    }
}
?>
```

4. **User Profile View** (views/user_profile.php):

php

```
<!DOCTYPE html>
<html lang="en">
<head>
  <meta charset="UTF-8">
  <title>User Profile</title>
</head>
<body>
  <h1>User Profile</h1>
  <?php if ($user): ?>
    <p>Name: <?php echo htmlspecialchars($user['name']); ?></p>
    <p>Email: <?php echo htmlspecialchars($user['email']); ?></p>
  <?php else: ?>
    <p>User not found.</p>
  <?php endif; ?>
</body>
</html>
```

5. **Index.php** (Application Entry Point):

php

```
<?php
```

```php
require_once 'config/database.php';
require_once 'models/User.php';
require_once 'controllers/UserController.php';

// Create database connection and model
$dbConnection = getDatabaseConnection();
$userModel = new User($dbConnection);

// Create controller and call the appropriate action
$userController = new UserController($userModel);

// For simplicity, let's assume we're getting the user ID
from the URL
$userId = isset($_GET['id']) ? (int)$_GET['id'] : 1;
$userController->showProfile($userId);
?>
```

Explanation of Flow:

1. **Index.php**: The application entry point, where we set up the database connection, initialize the Model and Controller, and determine the action (in this case, displaying the user profile).

2. **UserController**: The Controller calls the Model to retrieve data based on the user ID and passes it to the View.

3. **User Model**: The Model interacts with the database to fetch user information.

4. **User Profile View**: The View receives the data and displays it to the user.

Benefits of MVC in PHP Applications

Using MVC in PHP applications offers several advantages:

- **Modularity**: Components are separated, making it easier to update or replace them independently.
- **Reusability**: Models and Views can be reused in different parts of the application or even across projects.
- **Scalability**: The structured approach of MVC makes it easier to expand and manage large applications.
- **Maintainability**: Clear separation of concerns helps developers identify and fix issues more efficiently.

In this chapter, we introduced the Model-View-Controller (MVC) architecture and demonstrated how it can organize code in PHP applications. By separating data management, business logic, and presentation, MVC makes applications more modular, maintainable, and scalable. In the next chapter, we'll dive into using frameworks like Laravel, which build on the MVC pattern, to speed up PHP application development and provide even more robust tools for managing complex projects.

CHAPTER 14: ADVANCED SQL QUERIES AND OPTIMIZATION

1. Writing Complex SQL Queries

Complex queries are necessary for extracting specific information from your database, especially as data grows. Some common types of complex queries include **JOINs, subqueries, UNIONs**, and **aggregate functions**.

JOINs: Combining Data from Multiple Tables

JOINs are used to retrieve data from multiple tables in a single query, based on relationships between them.

1. **INNER JOIN**: Retrieves records with matching values in both tables.

   sql

   ```
   SELECT orders.id, customers.name, orders.total
   FROM orders
   INNER JOIN customers ON orders.customer_id = customers.id;
   ```

   This query fetches all orders along with the customer name by matching customer_id in orders with id in customers.

2. **LEFT JOIN**: Retrieves all records from the left table and matching records from the right table (NULL if there's no match).

sql

```
SELECT customers.name, orders.total
FROM customers
LEFT JOIN orders ON customers.id = orders.customer_id;
```

3. **RIGHT JOIN**: Retrieves all records from the right table and matching records from the left table (NULL if there's no match).

Subqueries: Queries within Queries

A **subquery** is a query nested within another query. Subqueries are helpful for filtering results based on a secondary dataset.

Example: Fetching customers with orders totaling more than $500.

sql

```
SELECT name
FROM customers
WHERE id IN (
    SELECT customer_id
    FROM orders
```

```
GROUP BY customer_id
HAVING SUM(total) > 500
```
);

In this example:

- The inner query retrieves customer_ids where the total order amount exceeds $500.
- The outer query retrieves customer names based on those IDs.

UNION: Combining Results from Multiple Queries

The **UNION** operator combines results from multiple SELECT statements into a single result set, removing duplicates.

Example: Retrieve all unique product names from products and services tables.

sql

```
SELECT name FROM products
UNION
SELECT name FROM services;
```

Use **UNION ALL** to keep duplicate rows:

sql

```
SELECT name FROM products
```

UNION ALL

SELECT name FROM services;

2. Aggregate Functions and Grouping

Aggregate functions perform calculations on data, often used with the **GROUP BY** clause.

1. **COUNT()**: Counts the number of rows in a group.

   sql

   ```
   SELECT customer_id, COUNT(*) AS order_count
   FROM orders
   GROUP BY customer_id;
   ```

2. **SUM()**: Returns the total sum of a numeric column.

   sql

   ```
   SELECT customer_id, SUM(total) AS total_spent
   FROM orders
   GROUP BY customer_id;
   ```

3. **AVG()**: Calculates the average value of a numeric column.

   sql

   ```
   SELECT product_id, AVG(price) AS average_price
   ```

FROM products

GROUP BY product_id;

4. **HAVING Clause**: Filters results after aggregation, often used with GROUP BY.

   Example: Retrieve products with an average price greater than $50.

   sql

   SELECT product_id, AVG(price) AS average_price
   FROM products
   GROUP BY product_id
   HAVING average_price > 50;

3. Indexing for Performance Optimization

Indexes are database structures that improve the speed of data retrieval operations. By creating an index on a column, MySQL can quickly locate rows without scanning the entire table. However, indexes also increase storage requirements and can slow down INSERT, UPDATE, and DELETE operations.

Types of Indexes

1. **Primary Index**: Automatically created for the primary key column(s). Uniquely identifies each row.

2. **Unique Index**: Ensures that all values in the indexed column are unique.

sql

CREATE UNIQUE INDEX idx_email ON users(email);

3. **Composite Index**: An index on multiple columns, useful for queries that filter based on more than one column.

sql

CREATE INDEX idx_customer_order ON orders(customer_id, order_date);

Best Practices for Indexing

- **Index Columns in WHERE Clauses**: Index columns frequently used in WHERE clauses to improve query speed.
- **Use Composite Indexes for Multi-Column Searches**: If a query filters by two or more columns, a composite index can speed it up.
- **Avoid Over-Indexing**: Indexes consume storage and slow down write operations. Only index columns that improve query performance.
- **Monitor Index Usage**: Use EXPLAIN to see if MySQL uses the index in a query.

4. Query Optimization Techniques

Optimizing queries is essential for maintaining database performance, especially with large datasets. Here are some techniques to optimize queries in MySQL:

1. Use EXPLAIN to Analyze Queries

The EXPLAIN statement helps analyze how MySQL executes a query, showing the order of tables accessed, indexes used, and estimated rows scanned.

sql

EXPLAIN SELECT * FROM orders WHERE customer_id = 5;

Look for the following in the EXPLAIN output:

- **type**: The join type (e.g., ALL, index, range, ref, const). ALL (full table scan) is the least efficient, while const is the most efficient.
- **key**: The index used for the query. If this is NULL, consider adding an index.

2. Limit Rows with WHERE and LIMIT

Narrow down result sets with WHERE conditions to reduce processing time. For example, fetching recent records with a LIMIT clause:

sql

SELECT * FROM orders WHERE order_date > '2023-01-01'
LIMIT 100;

3. Avoid Using SELECT *

Fetching all columns is often unnecessary and inefficient. Only
retrieve columns you need.

sql

```
-- Instead of:
SELECT * FROM users;
```

```
-- Use:
SELECT name, email FROM users;
```

4. Optimize Joins and Subqueries

1. **Use JOINs Instead of Subqueries**: JOINs are often faster
   than subqueries because MySQL optimizes them better.

   sql

   ```
   SELECT customers.name, orders.total
   FROM customers
   JOIN orders ON customers.id = orders.customer_id;
   ```

2. **Index Columns Used in JOINs**: Ensure columns used in JOINs are indexed for faster lookups.

5. Avoid Functions in WHERE Clauses

Functions in the WHERE clause prevent MySQL from using indexes effectively, as they alter the column value in each row. Instead of using functions, try to structure queries differently.

Example: Optimize a query that uses YEAR() by changing it to a range.

sql

```
-- Less efficient:
SELECT * FROM orders WHERE YEAR(order_date) = 2023;

-- More efficient:
SELECT * FROM orders WHERE order_date BETWEEN '2023-01-01' AND '2023-12-31';
```

6. Use Derived Tables for Complex Calculations

Derived tables (subqueries within the FROM clause) can reduce query complexity by calculating intermediate results.

Example: Calculate average product prices within each category and filter results.

sql

```
SELECT category, AVG(price) AS avg_price
FROM (
    SELECT category, price
    FROM products
) AS derived
GROUP BY category
HAVING avg_price > 100;
```

5. Caching and Temporary Tables

Caching and temporary tables can improve performance by storing frequently accessed data or intermediate results.

Query Caching

MySQL's query cache stores the results of select queries and reuses them for identical queries, reducing query processing time. Note that the query cache is effective for static or infrequently changing data.

To enable query caching in MySQL, set the following in my.cnf (MySQL's configuration file):

ini

```
query_cache_size = 256M
query_cache_type = 1
```

Temporary Tables

Temporary tables store intermediate results, especially useful in complex calculations or multi-step queries.

sql

```
CREATE TEMPORARY TABLE recent_orders AS
SELECT * FROM orders WHERE order_date > NOW() -
INTERVAL 30 DAY;

SELECT * FROM recent_orders WHERE total > 500;
```

Explanation:

- The temporary table recent_orders stores orders from the last 30 days.
- A second query retrieves high-value orders from this temporary table.

Temporary tables are automatically dropped when the session ends, reducing clutter in the database.

6. Monitoring and Tuning MySQL Performance

To ensure optimal database performance, monitoring and tuning MySQL settings is essential.

1. MySQL Slow Query Log

The Slow Query Log records queries that exceed a specified execution time, helping you identify slow queries for optimization.

Enable the Slow Query Log by adding the following to my.cnf:

ini

slow_query_log = 1
slow_query_log_file = /var/log/mysql/slow_queries.log
long_query_time = 2   # Log queries that take longer than 2 seconds

2. Adjust Key Buffer Size

The key buffer holds index blocks for MyISAM tables in memory, reducing the need to access the disk. For InnoDB, adjust the InnoDB buffer pool instead.

ini

key_buffer_size = 512M

3. Optimize Table Storage Engines

Choose the appropriate storage engine for your tables:

- **InnoDB**: Ideal for high-concurrency applications, supports transactions, and ensures data integrity.
- **MyISAM**: Faster for read-heavy workloads but lacks transaction support.

sql

```
ALTER TABLE orders ENGINE = InnoDB;
```

In this chapter, we covered advanced SQL techniques, including JOINs, subqueries, and aggregate functions, and we explored MySQL optimization strategies, such as indexing, query tuning, and caching. By implementing these practices, you can significantly improve the performance and scalability of your database, ensuring that it can handle large volumes of data efficiently. In the next chapter, we'll look into database security best practices, focusing on securing MySQL and protecting your application data from unauthorized access.

CHAPTER 15: BUILDING USER AUTHENTICATION SYSTEMS

1. Designing the Authentication Workflow

The authentication workflow generally involves these steps:

1. **User Registration**: Users provide information, such as a username and password, which are securely stored in the database.

2. **Login**: Users enter their credentials, which the system verifies against stored data.

3. **Session Management**: Once authenticated, the user's session is tracked, allowing access to protected pages.

4. **Logout**: Ends the session and redirects the user to a public page.

2. Creating the Database Structure

Let's start by creating a users table in MySQL to store user information securely.

sql

```
CREATE DATABASE auth_system;
USE auth_system;
```

```
CREATE TABLE users (
    id INT AUTO_INCREMENT PRIMARY KEY,
    username VARCHAR(50) NOT NULL UNIQUE,
    email VARCHAR(100) NOT NULL UNIQUE,
    password VARCHAR(255) NOT NULL,
    created_at              TIMESTAMP              DEFAULT
CURRENT_TIMESTAMP
);
```

Explanation:

- **id**: A unique identifier for each user.
- **username and email**: User credentials, set to be unique to prevent duplicates.
- **password**: Stores the user's hashed password for security.
- **created_at**: Records when the user registered.

3. Secure Password Storage with Hashing

To protect passwords, we hash them before storing them in the database. PHP's password_hash() function provides a secure way to hash passwords with the bcrypt algorithm, making it difficult to reverse-engineer.

Hashing a Password

php

```php
<?php
$password = "userpassword";
$hashedPassword = password_hash($password,
PASSWORD_BCRYPT);
echo $hashedPassword;
?>
```

Explanation:

- **password_hash()**: Generates a hashed version of the password. The PASSWORD_BCRYPT option uses bcrypt, a strong hashing algorithm suitable for password security.

Verifying a Password

When users log in, we use password_verify() to compare the entered password with the stored hash.

php

```php
<?php
$enteredPassword = "userpassword";
if (password_verify($enteredPassword, $hashedPassword)) {
    echo "Password is correct!";
} else {
    echo "Invalid password.";
}
?>
```

Explanation:

- **password_verify()**: Checks if the entered password matches the hashed password. This prevents storing or exposing plain-text passwords.

4. Building the Registration System

Let's create a registration form where users can create an account. We'll handle form submission, validate input, hash the password, and store the user's information in the database.

1. **HTML Form for User Registration**:

html

```html
<!DOCTYPE html>
<html lang="en">
<head>
    <meta charset="UTF-8">
    <title>Register</title>
</head>
<body>
    <h2>Register</h2>
    <form action="register.php" method="POST">
        <label for="username">Username:</label>
        <input type="text" id="username" name="username" required>
```

```html
    <label for="email">Email:</label>
    <input type="email" id="email" name="email"
required>
    <label for="password">Password:</label>
    <input type="password" id="password"
name="password" required>
    <button type="submit">Register</button>
  </form>
</body>
</html>
```

2. **PHP Script to Handle Registration (register.php)**:

php

```php
<?php
include 'config/database.php';

if ($_SERVER["REQUEST_METHOD"] == "POST") {
   $username = $_POST['username'];
   $email = $_POST['email'];
   $password = $_POST['password'];

   // Hash the password
   $hashedPassword = password_hash($password,
PASSWORD_BCRYPT);
```

```php
// Insert user data into the database
$stmt = $conn->prepare("INSERT INTO users
(username, email, password) VALUES (?, ?, ?)");
$stmt->bind_param("sss", $username, $email,
$hashedPassword);

if ($stmt->execute()) {
    echo "Registration successful!";
} else {
    echo "Error: " . $stmt->error;
}

$stmt->close();
$conn->close();
}
?>
```

Explanation:

- **Data Validation**: We retrieve and sanitize form data.
- **Password Hashing**: We hash the password with password_hash() before storing it.
- **SQL Insert**: The user's details, including the hashed password, are inserted into the users table.

5. Building the Login System

The login system verifies the user's credentials, and if correct, initiates a session to track the user.

1. **HTML Form for Login**:

html

```
<!DOCTYPE html>
<html lang="en">
<head>
    <meta charset="UTF-8">
    <title>Login</title>
</head>
<body>
    <h2>Login</h2>
    <form action="login.php" method="POST">
        <label for="username">Username:</label>
        <input type="text" id="username" name="username" required>
        <label for="password">Password:</label>
        <input type="password" id="password" name="password" required>
        <button type="submit">Login</button>
    </form>
</body>
</html>
```

2. **PHP Script to Handle Login (login.php)**:

php

```php
<?php
session_start();
include 'config/database.php';

if ($_SERVER["REQUEST_METHOD"] == "POST") {
    $username = $_POST['username'];
    $password = $_POST['password'];

    // Retrieve user record by username
    $stmt = $conn->prepare("SELECT id, password FROM
users WHERE username = ?");
    $stmt->bind_param("s", $username);
    $stmt->execute();
    $stmt->bind_result($id, $hashedPassword);
    $stmt->fetch();

    if ($hashedPassword && password_verify($password,
$hashedPassword)) {
        // Set session variables
        $_SESSION['user_id'] = $id;
        $_SESSION['username'] = $username;
        header("Location: dashboard.php");
```

```
        exit;
    } else {
        echo "Invalid username or password.";
    }

    $stmt->close();
    $conn->close();
}
?>
```

Explanation:

- **Password Verification**: We use password_verify() to check if the entered password matches the stored hash.
- **Session Management**: On successful login, session variables (user_id and username) are set to track the user's session.

6. Protecting Pages with Authentication

After logging in, we can protect specific pages by verifying if the user session is active.

Example: A protected dashboard page (dashboard.php).

php

```
<?php
session_start();
```

```php
if (!isset($_SESSION['user_id'])) {
    header("Location: login.php");
    exit;
}
?>


<!DOCTYPE html>
<html lang="en">
<head>
    <meta charset="UTF-8">
    <title>Dashboard</title>
</head>
<body>
    <h1>Welcome, <?php echo htmlspecialchars($_SESSION['username']); ?>!</h1>
    <p>This is your dashboard. Only logged-in users can see this page.</p>
    <a href="logout.php">Logout</a>
</body>
</html>
```

Explanation:

- **Session Check**: If user_id is not set in the session, the user is redirected to login.php.
- **Displaying User Info**: The dashboard page uses the session variable username to display the user's name.

7. Logging Out

Logging out ends the session, removing all session data.

PHP Script to Handle Logout (logout.php):

php

```php
<?php
session_start();
session_unset();   // Remove all session variables
session_destroy(); // Destroy the session

header("Location: login.php");
exit;
?>
```

Explanation:

- **session_unset()**: Clears all session variables.
- **session_destroy()**: Destroys the session, logging the user out.

8. Security Best Practices for Authentication

Security is crucial when handling user authentication. Here are some best practices:

1. **Use HTTPS**: Encrypt data transmitted between the client and server by implementing HTTPS, especially when handling sensitive information like passwords.

2. **Password Hashing**: Always hash passwords using password_hash() and verify with password_verify() to prevent storing plain-text passwords.

3. **Limit Login Attempts**: Implement a limit on login attempts to prevent brute-force attacks.

4. **Session Hijacking Prevention**:

   o **Regenerate Session ID**: Use session_regenerate_id() on login to prevent session fixation attacks.

   o **Set Secure Cookie Flags**: Use the secure and httponly flags for session cookies to protect against session hijacking.

5. **SQL Injection Prevention**: Always use prepared statements to protect against SQL injection attacks.

In this chapter, we built a secure user authentication system using PHP and MySQL, covering registration, login, session management, and logout. By hashing passwords, implementing secure session management, and following best practices, you can create an authentication system that protects user data and prevents unauthorized access. In the next chapter, we'll explore email verification and password reset functionalities, extending the authentication system to improve user experience and security further.

CHAPTER 16: SECURING YOUR PHP APPLICATIONS

1. Understanding Common Security Vulnerabilities

Before we dive into specific security measures, let's outline some of the most common security threats for PHP applications:

1. **SQL Injection**: An attack where malicious SQL code is injected into a query, potentially exposing or corrupting data.
2. **Cross-Site Scripting (XSS)**: Allows attackers to inject malicious scripts into webpages viewed by other users.
3. **Cross-Site Request Forgery (CSRF)**: Tricks a user into performing actions on a website where they're authenticated.
4. **Session Hijacking**: An attacker gains unauthorized access to a user's session.
5. **Data Exposure**: Sensitive data (like passwords) is stored or transmitted insecurely, potentially exposing it to attackers.

Let's explore how to mitigate each of these risks.

2. Preventing SQL Injection

SQL injection occurs when untrusted input is inserted directly into an SQL query. Attackers can manipulate queries, potentially accessing or destroying data. To prevent SQL injection:

1. Use Prepared Statements and Parameterized Queries

Prepared statements ensure that user input is treated as data, not executable SQL code, making them the most effective defense against SQL injection.

Example: Using prepared statements with MySQLi

php

```php
<?php
include 'config/database.php';

$username = $_POST['username'];
$password = $_POST['password'];

$stmt = $conn->prepare("SELECT * FROM users WHERE username = ? AND password = ?");
$stmt->bind_param("ss", $username, $password); // "ss" indicates two string parameters
$stmt->execute();
$result = $stmt->get_result();

if ($result->num_rows > 0) {
    echo "User authenticated successfully.";
} else {
    echo "Invalid username or password.";
```

```
}
?>
```

Explanation:

- **Parameterized Query**: ? placeholders are used in the SQL query to separate SQL code from data.
- **bind_param()**: Binds user input to these placeholders, preventing it from being executed as SQL.

2. Avoid Dynamic SQL

Avoid constructing SQL queries by concatenating strings and user inputs. Dynamic SQL allows attackers to inject malicious code.

php

```php
// Unsafe:
$sql = "SELECT * FROM users WHERE username = '" . $_POST['username'] . "'";
```

Instead, always use prepared statements to keep SQL and data separate.

---

3. Preventing Cross-Site Scripting (XSS)

XSS attacks occur when attackers inject malicious scripts into webpages, often through forms or URL parameters. When unsuspecting users visit the page, the script executes in their browsers, potentially stealing cookies or redirecting them.

1. Sanitize User Input

Use PHP's htmlspecialchars() function to escape special HTML characters, preventing the input from being interpreted as code.

Example:

php

```php
<?php
$userInput = "<script>alert('XSS');</script>";
$safeOutput = htmlspecialchars($userInput, ENT_QUOTES, 'UTF-8');
echo $safeOutput;  // Outputs: &lt;script&gt;alert('XSS');&lt;/script&gt;
?>
```

Explanation:

- **htmlspecialchars()**: Converts special characters like < and > into HTML entities, preventing them from executing as code in the browser.

2. Sanitize Output Before Rendering HTML

Whenever displaying user input on the page, sanitize it. Use htmlspecialchars() or strip_tags() to ensure it's safe for display.

Example in an HTML context:

php

```
<p><?php echo htmlspecialchars($user['name'], ENT_QUOTES, 'UTF-8'); ?></p>
```

---

4. Preventing Cross-Site Request Forgery (CSRF)

CSRF attacks occur when an attacker tricks a user into performing an action they didn't intend. For example, a malicious link could submit a form on behalf of the user. To protect against CSRF:

1. Use CSRF Tokens

A CSRF token is a unique, random value included in forms and validated upon submission, ensuring that the request came from an authorized source.

1. **Generate and Store the CSRF Token:**

php

```
session_start();
if (empty($_SESSION['csrf_token'])) {
    $_SESSION['csrf_token'] = bin2hex(random_bytes(32));
// Generate a random CSRF token
}
```

2. **Add CSRF Token to Form**:

html

```html
<form action="process.php" method="POST">
    <input type="hidden" name="csrf_token" value="<?php echo $_SESSION['csrf_token']; ?>">
    <!-- Other form fields -->
    <button type="submit">Submit</button>
</form>
```

3. **Validate the CSRF Token on Form Submission**:

php

```php
session_start();
if ($_SERVER["REQUEST_METHOD"] == "POST") {
    if          (hash_equals($_SESSION['csrf_token'], $_POST['csrf_token'])) {
        // Process form
    } else {
        die("CSRF token validation failed.");
    }
}
```

Explanation:

- The token is added as a hidden field in the form and compared with the session's token upon submission.
- **hash_equals()**: Compares tokens securely, preventing timing attacks.

5. Securing Session Management

Sessions store user-specific data across different pages, often used for login states. Securing sessions is essential to prevent session hijacking.

1. Use HTTPS for Encrypted Communication

Ensure that your application runs on HTTPS to protect session data from being intercepted.

2. Regenerate Session ID Upon Login

Regenerating the session ID after a successful login prevents session fixation attacks, where an attacker forces a known session ID on a user.

php

```
session_start();
session_regenerate_id(true); // Generate a new session ID
$_SESSION['user_id'] = $userId;
```

3. Set Secure Session Cookies

Enable the httponly and secure flags for cookies to prevent client-side access and ensure they are sent only over HTTPS.

php

```
session_set_cookie_params([
    'httponly' => true,
    'secure' => true,
    'samesite' => 'Strict'
]);
session_start();
```

6. Protecting Sensitive Data

Protecting sensitive information, such as passwords and user data, is critical for a secure application.

1. Hash Passwords Using Strong Algorithms

Use password_hash() for hashing passwords and password_verify() for checking them, as these functions handle salt and algorithm management.

Example:

php

```
$hashedPassword        =        password_hash($userPassword,
PASSWORD_BCRYPT);
if (password_verify($enteredPassword, $hashedPassword)) {
    // Password is valid
}
```

2. Encrypt Sensitive Data at Rest

For highly sensitive information, such as payment details, consider encrypting data at rest using strong encryption libraries like openssl_encrypt().

Example:

php

```
$key = "your-encryption-key"; // Use a secure key management strategy
$encryptedData = openssl_encrypt($data, 'aes-256-cbc', $key, 0, $iv);
```

7. *Limiting File Uploads*

File uploads pose security risks if not managed correctly. Attackers can upload malicious files disguised as images or other types. Here's how to secure file uploads:

1. Validate File Types

Only allow specific file types, like images, by checking the MIME type.

php

```
$allowedTypes = ["image/jpeg", "image/png", "image/gif"];
```

```php
if    (!in_array(mime_content_type($_FILES['file']['tmp_name'])),
$allowedTypes)) {
    die("Invalid file type.");
}
```

2. Limit File Size

Set a maximum file size to prevent excessively large files that could overload the server.

php

```php
if ($_FILES['file']['size'] > 2 * 1024 * 1024) { // 2MB limit
    die("File is too large.");
}
```

3. Rename Files on Upload

Rename files to unique names to prevent overwriting and avoid using user input in filenames.

php

```php
$newFileName       =       uniqid()       .       "_"       .
basename($_FILES['file']['name']);
move_uploaded_file($_FILES['file']['tmp_name'],    "uploads/"    .
$newFileName);
```

---

8. Implementing Secure Error Handling

Error messages can expose sensitive information, such as SQL queries or file paths. To avoid leaking information:

- **Hide Error Messages from Users**: In production, disable error display and log errors to a file instead.

php

```
ini_set('display_errors', 0);
ini_set('log_errors', 1);
ini_set('error_log', '/path/to/php-error.log');
```

- **Custom Error Pages**: Redirect users to a custom error page instead of showing raw error messages.

9. Best Practices for Secure Coding

1. **Sanitize Input and Escape Output**: Always sanitize input and escape output to prevent SQL injection and XSS.
2. **Use Modern Libraries**: Use trusted libraries and frameworks that follow secure practices, such as Laravel, which provides CSRF protection, XSS prevention, and built-in security mechanisms.
3. **Keep Software Updated**: Regularly update PHP, MySQL, and libraries to ensure you have the latest security patches.

4. **Principle of Least Privilege**: Grant only the permissions needed for each user and process. For example, database accounts should have the minimum required privileges.

In this chapter, we covered essential security practices for protecting PHP applications, including preventing SQL injection and XSS, implementing CSRF protection, securing session management, and safeguarding sensitive data. By following these practices, you can significantly reduce the risk of security breaches and protect both your application and your users. In the next chapter, we'll look into API integration, focusing on how to securely connect PHP applications with external services and handle sensitive API data.

CHAPTER 17: AJAX AND PHP FOR ASYNCHRONOUS APPLICATIONS

1. Introduction to AJAX

AJAX is not a programming language but a technique that combines JavaScript, HTML, and XML or JSON to communicate with a server asynchronously. By using AJAX, web applications can:

- Retrieve data from the server without reloading the entire page.
- Send data to the server in response to user interactions (like form submissions).
- Dynamically update only specific parts of a webpage.

Modern AJAX requests typically use **XMLHttpRequest** or the **Fetch API** to handle asynchronous data exchanges with the server.

2. Setting Up an AJAX Request with JavaScript

Let's start by creating a basic AJAX setup where JavaScript sends a request to a PHP script, and the PHP script returns data that we display dynamically on the page.

Example: Simple AJAX Request to Fetch Data

Suppose we want to create a feature where clicking a button fetches a random quote from the server.

1. **HTML and JavaScript**:

   html

```html
<!DOCTYPE html>
<html lang="en">
<head>
    <meta charset="UTF-8">
    <title>Random Quote</title>
    <script>
        function fetchQuote() {
            const xhr = new XMLHttpRequest();
            xhr.open("GET", "get_quote.php", true);

            xhr.onload = function() {
                if (xhr.status === 200) {
```

```
document.getElementById("quote").innerHTML          =
xhr.responseText;
            }
        };

        xhr.send();
    }
    </script>
</head>
<body>
    <h1>Random Quote Generator</h1>
    <button onclick="fetchQuote()">Get Quote</button>
    <p id="quote"></p>
</body>
</html>
```

2. **PHP Script (get_quote.php)**:

php

```
<?php
$quotes = [
    "The only limit to our realization of tomorrow is our
doubts of today.",
```

```
    "Success is not final, failure is not fatal: It is the courage
to continue that counts.",
    "Life is what happens when you're busy making other
plans.",
    "Believe you can and you're halfway there."
];

// Select a random quote
$randomQuote = $quotes[array_rand($quotes)];

echo $randomQuote;
?>
```

Explanation:

- **JavaScript AJAX Request**: The fetchQuote() function creates an XMLHttpRequest, sends it to get_quote.php, and displays the response in the <p id="quote"> element.
- **PHP Script**: get_quote.php randomly selects a quote from an array and returns it as the response text.

When the button is clicked, the AJAX request is sent to the server, and the quote is fetched and displayed asynchronously without reloading the page.

3. AJAX with Form Data: Sending and Receiving Data

In addition to fetching data, AJAX is often used to send data to the server (e.g., form submissions) without reloading the page. Let's create a form that sends data to a PHP script using AJAX and displays a success message.

Example: AJAX Form Submission

1. **HTML and JavaScript**:

html

```html
<!DOCTYPE html>
<html lang="en">
<head>
   <meta charset="UTF-8">
   <title>Contact Form</title>
   <script>
     function submitForm() {
       const xhr = new XMLHttpRequest();
       const formData = new FormData(document.getElementById("contactForm"));

       xhr.open("POST", "submit_form.php", true);

       xhr.onload = function() {
         if (xhr.status === 200) {
```

PHP and MySQL Web Development

```
        document.getElementById("formMessage").innerHTML =
        xhr.responseText;
                }
            };

            xhr.send(formData);
        }
    </script>
</head>
<body>
    <h1>Contact Us</h1>
    <form                               id="contactForm"
onsubmit="event.preventDefault(); submitForm();">
        <label for="name">Name:</label>
        <input    type="text"    id="name"    name="name"
required>
        <label for="email">Email:</label>
        <input   type="email"   id="email"   name="email"
required>
        <button type="submit">Submit</button>
    </form>
    <p id="formMessage"></p>
</body>
</html>
```

2. **PHP Script to Process the Form (submit_form.php)**:

php

```php
<?php
if ($_SERVER["REQUEST_METHOD"] == "POST") {
    $name = htmlspecialchars($_POST['name']);
    $email = htmlspecialchars($_POST['email']);

    // Assume form submission is successful
    echo "Thank you, $name! We have received your message.";
} else {
    echo "Invalid request.";
}
?>
```

Explanation:

- **JavaScript Form Submission**: When the form is submitted, submitForm() creates a FormData object containing the form fields and values. The AJAX request sends the data to submit_form.php via POST, and the server's response is displayed.
- **PHP Script**: submit_form.php processes the form, sanitizes the input with htmlspecialchars(), and sends a confirmation message back.

4. Using AJAX with the Fetch API

The Fetch API provides a modern, more readable way to handle AJAX requests compared to XMLHttpRequest. Here's how to rewrite the previous example using Fetch.

Example: Fetch API for Form Submission

1. **HTML and JavaScript**:

html

```
<!DOCTYPE html>
<html lang="en">
<head>
    <meta charset="UTF-8">
    <title>Contact Form with Fetch</title>
    <script>
        async function submitForm() {
            const formData = new FormData(document.getElementById("contactForm"));
            const response = await fetch("submit_form.php", {
                method: "POST",
                body: formData
            });

            const result = await response.text();
```

```
document.getElementById("formMessage").innerHTML =
result;
    }
  </script>
</head>
<body>
  <h1>Contact Us</h1>
  <form                                    id="contactForm"
onsubmit="event.preventDefault(); submitForm();">
    <label for="name">Name:</label>
    <input   type="text"   id="name"   name="name"
required>
    <label for="email">Email:</label>
    <input   type="email"   id="email"   name="email"
required>
    <button type="submit">Submit</button>
  </form>
  <p id="formMessage"></p>
</body>
</html>
```

Explanation:

- **Fetch API**: The fetch() method sends the form data to submit_form.php using POST. We handle the response asynchronously with await, making the code more readable.

5. Returning JSON Data with AJAX and PHP

JSON (JavaScript Object Notation) is a lightweight data format commonly used with AJAX because it's easy to parse in JavaScript.

Example: Fetching JSON Data

Suppose we want to create an API that returns user information in JSON format.

1. **JavaScript to Fetch JSON**:

   html

   ```html
   <script>
       async function fetchUser() {
           const response = await fetch("get_user.php");
           const data = await response.json();
           document.getElementById("userInfo").innerHTML =
   `Name: ${data.name}, Email: ${data.email}`;
           }
   </script>

   <button onclick="fetchUser()">Get User Info</button>
   <p id="userInfo"></p>
   ```

2. **PHP Script to Generate JSON (get_user.php)**:

   php

```php
<?php
header("Content-Type: application/json");

$user = [
    "name" => "John Doe",
    "email" => "john@example.com"
];

echo json_encode($user);
?>
```

Explanation:

- **JavaScript**: fetchUser() sends an AJAX request to get_user.php, parses the JSON response, and displays it.
- **PHP Script**: get_user.php sets the Content-Type to application/json and uses json_encode() to send the data in JSON format.

6. Common AJAX Use Cases

AJAX enables various interactive features without reloading the page. Here are some common use cases:

1. **Live Search Suggestions**: Display search suggestions as the user types by sending each keystroke to the server and retrieving matching results.

2. **Form Validation**: Validate form inputs (like username availability) in real-time without page reload.

3. **Infinite Scrolling and Pagination**: Load additional content as the user scrolls down, creating an infinite scroll experience.

4. **Real-Time Chat Applications**: Retrieve and display messages from the server continuously to create live chat interfaces.

5. **Updating Cart or Wishlist**: Update shopping cart items or wishlists in real-time without reloading the page.

7. Security Considerations for AJAX

While AJAX enhances user experience, it introduces potential security risks. Here are some best practices:

- **Input Validation**: Always validate and sanitize input on the server, as users can manipulate AJAX requests.

- **CSRF Protection**: Use CSRF tokens to protect sensitive actions (like updating data) performed with AJAX.

- **JSON Hijacking Prevention**: When returning JSON data, use Content-Type: application/json headers to prevent malicious scripts from reading data.

- **Access Control**: Ensure only authorized users can access specific AJAX endpoints by validating sessions or authentication tokens.

In this chapter, we explored how to create dynamic, asynchronous applications using AJAX and PHP. By leveraging AJAX requests, you can improve user experience by loading content dynamically without refreshing the entire page. We covered basic AJAX requests, form submission, and working with JSON data, along with some best practices for security. In the next chapter, we'll dive into API integration, focusing on how to connect PHP applications with external APIs and process JSON data securely.

CHAPTER 18: DEVELOPING A CONTENT MANAGEMENT SYSTEM (CMS)

1. Setting Up the CMS Database Structure

Let's start by setting up the MySQL database structure to support articles, users, and comments. Each table is designed to handle essential relationships between content, users, and feedback.

Database Schema

1. **Database Creation**:

   sql

```
CREATE DATABASE cms;
USE cms;
```

2. **Users Table**: Stores user information.

sql

```
CREATE TABLE users (
    id INT AUTO_INCREMENT PRIMARY KEY,
    username VARCHAR(50) NOT NULL UNIQUE,
    email VARCHAR(100) NOT NULL UNIQUE,
    password VARCHAR(255) NOT NULL,
    role ENUM('admin', 'author', 'subscriber') DEFAULT 'subscriber',
    created_at TIMESTAMP DEFAULT CURRENT_TIMESTAMP
);
```

3. **Articles Table**: Stores articles written by users.

sql

```
CREATE TABLE articles (
    id INT AUTO_INCREMENT PRIMARY KEY,
    user_id INT NOT NULL,
    title VARCHAR(255) NOT NULL,
    content TEXT NOT NULL,
```

```sql
    created_at          TIMESTAMP           DEFAULT
CURRENT_TIMESTAMP,
    FOREIGN KEY (user_id) REFERENCES users(id) ON
DELETE CASCADE
);
```

4. **Comments Table**: Stores comments on articles.

sql

```sql
CREATE TABLE comments (
    id INT AUTO_INCREMENT PRIMARY KEY,
    article_id INT NOT NULL,
    user_id INT NOT NULL,
    comment TEXT NOT NULL,
    created_at          TIMESTAMP           DEFAULT
CURRENT_TIMESTAMP,
    FOREIGN KEY (article_id) REFERENCES articles(id)
ON DELETE CASCADE,
    FOREIGN KEY (user_id) REFERENCES users(id) ON
DELETE CASCADE
);
```

Explanation:

- **users** table: Stores user credentials, email, password, and user roles.

- **articles** table: Stores articles with relationships to the author's user ID.
- **comments** table: Stores comments with relationships to the article ID and user ID.

2. User Registration and Login

We'll begin by implementing user registration and login functionality, which is foundational for any CMS. Each user will be able to register, log in, and be assigned a role.

User Registration Form

1. **HTML Form** (register.html):

html

```
<!DOCTYPE html>
<html lang="en">
<head>
    <meta charset="UTF-8">
    <title>Register</title>
</head>
<body>
    <h2>Register</h2>
    <form action="register.php" method="POST">
        <label for="username">Username:</label>
```

```html
    <input type="text" id="username" name="username"
required>
    <label for="email">Email:</label>
    <input type="email" id="email" name="email"
required>
    <label for="password">Password:</label>
    <input type="password" id="password"
name="password" required>
    <button type="submit">Register</button>
  </form>
</body>
</html>
```

2. **PHP Script to Handle Registration** (register.php):

php

```php
<?php
include 'config/database.php';

if ($_SERVER["REQUEST_METHOD"] == "POST") {
  $username = $_POST['username'];
  $email = $_POST['email'];
  $password = password_hash($_POST['password'],
PASSWORD_BCRYPT);
```

```php
$stmt = $conn->prepare("INSERT INTO users
(username, email, password) VALUES (?, ?, ?)");
$stmt->bind_param("sss", $username, $email,
$password);

if ($stmt->execute()) {
    echo "Registration successful!";
} else {
    echo "Error: " . $stmt->error;
}

$stmt->close();
$conn->close();
}
?>
```

User Login Form

1. **HTML Form** (login.html):

html

```html
<!DOCTYPE html>
<html lang="en">
<head>
    <meta charset="UTF-8">
```

```html
    <title>Login</title>
</head>
<body>
    <h2>Login</h2>
    <form action="login.php" method="POST">
        <label for="username">Username:</label>
        <input type="text" id="username" name="username" required>
        <label for="password">Password:</label>
        <input type="password" id="password" name="password" required>
        <button type="submit">Login</button>
    </form>
</body>
</html>
```

2. **PHP Script to Handle Login** (login.php):

php

```php
<?php
session_start();
include 'config/database.php';

if ($_SERVER["REQUEST_METHOD"] == "POST") {
    $username = $_POST['username'];
```

```php
$password = $_POST['password'];

$stmt = $conn->prepare("SELECT id, password, role FROM users WHERE username = ?");
$stmt->bind_param("s", $username);
$stmt->execute();
$stmt->bind_result($id, $hashedPassword, $role);
$stmt->fetch();

if ($hashedPassword && password_verify($password, $hashedPassword)) {
    $_SESSION['user_id'] = $id;
    $_SESSION['username'] = $username;
    $_SESSION['role'] = $role;
    header("Location: dashboard.php");
    exit;
} else {
    echo "Invalid username or password.";
}

$stmt->close();
$conn->close();
}
?>
```

Explanation:

- The login and registration systems hash passwords securely using password_hash() and verify them with password_verify().

3. Creating and Managing Articles

Only authenticated users with appropriate roles can create, view, and manage articles. Let's set up functionality for creating and displaying articles.

Creating an Article

1. **Article Submission Form** (create_article.html):

html

```
<!DOCTYPE html>
<html lang="en">
<head>
    <meta charset="UTF-8">
    <title>Create Article</title>
</head>
<body>
    <h2>Create a New Article</h2>
    <form action="create_article.php" method="POST">
        <label for="title">Title:</label>
        <input type="text" id="title" name="title" required>
        <label for="content">Content:</label>
```

```
        <textarea        id="content"        name="content"
required></textarea>
        <button type="submit">Submit</button>
    </form>
</body>
</html>
```

2. **PHP Script to Handle Article Creation** (create_article.php):

php

```php
<?php
session_start();
include 'config/database.php';

if (!isset($_SESSION['user_id'])) {
    header("Location: login.html");
    exit;
}

if ($_SERVER["REQUEST_METHOD"] == "POST") {
    $title = $_POST['title'];
    $content = $_POST['content'];
    $userId = $_SESSION['user_id'];
```

```php
$stmt = $conn->prepare("INSERT INTO articles
(user_id, title, content) VALUES (?, ?, ?)");
$stmt->bind_param("iss", $userId, $title, $content);

if ($stmt->execute()) {
    echo "Article created successfully.";
} else {
    echo "Error: " . $stmt->error;
}

$stmt->close();
$conn->close();
}
?>
```

Explanation:

- **User Role Check**: Only logged-in users can create articles. Articles are associated with the user ID of the author.

4. Displaying Articles and Comments

Next, let's display articles with user comments.

1. **Displaying Articles with Comments** (view_article.php):

php

```php
<?php
```

```php
include 'config/database.php';

$articleId = $_GET['id'];
$stmt = $conn->prepare("SELECT title, content, created_at
FROM articles WHERE id = ?");
$stmt->bind_param("i", $articleId);
$stmt->execute();
$stmt->bind_result($title, $content, $createdAt);
$stmt->fetch();
?>


<!DOCTYPE html>
<html lang="en">
<head>
    <meta charset="UTF-8">
    <title><?php echo htmlspecialchars($title); ?></title>
</head>
<body>
    <h1><?php echo htmlspecialchars($title); ?></h1>
    <p><?php echo htmlspecialchars($content); ?></p>
    <small>Published    on:    <?php    echo    $createdAt;
?></small>

    <h2>Comments</h2>
    <?php
```

```php
$stmt->close();
$commentStmt = $conn->prepare("SELECT comment, created_at FROM comments WHERE article_id = ?");
$commentStmt->bind_param("i", $articleId);
$commentStmt->execute();
$commentStmt->bind_result($comment, $commentDate);

while ($commentStmt->fetch()) {
    echo "<p>" . htmlspecialchars($comment) . " <small>($commentDate)</small></p>";
}

$commentStmt->close();
$conn->close();
?>
</body>
</html>
```

5. Adding Comments

Users can add comments to articles.

Comment Form and Processing (add_comment.php):

1. **HTML for Comment Form**:

html

```
<form action="add_comment.php" method="POST">
    <textarea name="comment" required></textarea>
    <input type="hidden" name="article_id" value="<?php
echo $articleId; ?>">
    <button type="submit">Add Comment</button>
</form>
```

2. **PHP Script to Handle Comment Submission**:

php

```
<?php
session_start();
include 'config/database.php';

if ($_SERVER["REQUEST_METHOD"] == "POST" &&
isset($_SESSION['user_id'])) {
    $comment = $_POST['comment'];
    $articleId = $_POST['article_id'];
    $userId = $_SESSION['user_id'];

    $stmt = $conn->prepare("INSERT INTO comments
(article_id, user_id, comment) VALUES (?, ?, ?)");
    $stmt->bind_param("iis", $articleId, $userId,
$comment);
```

```php
if ($stmt->execute()) {
    header("Location: view_article.php?id=$articleId");
} else {
    echo "Error: " . $stmt->error;
}

$stmt->close();
$conn->close();
} else {
    echo "Unauthorized access.";
}
?>
```

Explanation:

- **User Authentication**: Comments can only be added by authenticated users.
- **Article Association**: Each comment is linked to a specific article.

6. Security Measures for the CMS

1. **SQL Injection Prevention**: Use prepared statements to prevent SQL injection attacks.
2. **Session Management**: Implement role-based access (e.g., only authors or admins can create articles).

3. **Input Sanitization**: Use htmlspecialchars() to sanitize output and prevent XSS attacks.

4. **Password Hashing**: Use password_hash() for secure password storage.

In this chapter, we built a basic CMS with PHP and MySQL, covering user registration, login, article creation, and comments. We also implemented basic security measures to protect the CMS from common vulnerabilities. With this foundation, you can expand the CMS with features like role-based permissions, article categories, or content moderation to suit specific needs. In the next chapter, we'll cover how to deploy this PHP application to a live server, preparing it for production.

CHAPTER 19: DEPLOYING PHP AND MYSQL APPLICATIONS

1. Choosing a Hosting Provider

To deploy a PHP and MySQL application, you need a hosting provider that supports:

- **PHP** (matching the version used in development)
- **MySQL** (or MariaDB) for database management
- **SSH/SFTP Access** for secure file transfers
- **cPanel** or **Plesk** (optional but helpful for easier server management)

Some popular hosting providers for PHP and MySQL applications include:

- **Shared Hosting**: Bluehost, SiteGround, HostGator
- **VPS Hosting**: DigitalOcean, Linode, Amazon Lightsail
- **Managed Hosting**: Cloudways (for managed cloud hosting)

2. Setting Up the Server Environment

Option 1: Shared Hosting

Most shared hosting providers come pre-configured with PHP and MySQL, making it simpler to set up. Typically, you'll access your server environment using **cPanel**, where you can manage files, databases, and server configurations.

1. **Log in to cPanel**: Access the cPanel dashboard from your hosting provider's website.

2. **File Manager**: Use the File Manager to upload your files or access them via FTP/SFTP.

3. **MySQL Databases**: Use the MySQL Databases section in cPanel to create databases and manage users.

Option 2: VPS or Dedicated Server

With a VPS or dedicated server, you have more control but need to configure PHP, MySQL, and Apache or Nginx manually.

1. **Install PHP and MySQL**:
   - On Ubuntu/Debian:

   bash

   ```
   sudo apt update
   sudo apt install php mysql-server apache2
   ```

   - On CentOS/RHEL:

   bash

   ```
   sudo yum install php mysql-server httpd
   ```

2. **Secure MySQL**: Run the MySQL security script to set up root passwords and secure MySQL.

bash

sudo mysql_secure_installation

3. **Enable and Start Services**:
   - Apache:

     bash

     ```
     sudo systemctl enable apache2
     sudo systemctl start apache2
     ```

   - MySQL:

     bash

     ```
     sudo systemctl enable mysql
     sudo systemctl start mysql
     ```

3. Preparing Your Application for Deployment

Before deploying your PHP application, make sure it's production-ready.

1. **Check PHP Version**: Ensure the PHP version on your server matches (or is compatible with) the version you used for development.

2. **Environment Configuration**: Set your application's configuration to production mode.

   - Disable error display in PHP by setting display_errors = Off in php.ini.
   - Enable logging to record errors without exposing them to users.

3. **Database Connection**: Update your database configuration to match the production database credentials.

   Example config/database.php:

   php

```php
<?php
$servername = "your_host";
$username = "your_database_user";
$password = "your_database_password";
$dbname = "your_database_name";

$conn = new mysqli($servername, $username, $password, $dbname);

if ($conn->connect_error) {
    die("Connection failed: " . $conn->connect_error);
}
?>
```

4. Transferring Files to the Server

You can upload your PHP files to the server using **FTP**, **SFTP**, or a **control panel like cPanel**.

1. **Using FTP/SFTP**:
    o   Install an FTP client (e.g., FileZilla).
    o   Connect to your server with your FTP credentials.
    o   Upload your files to the appropriate directory (usually public_html or www).

2. **Using cPanel's File Manager**:
    o   Log in to cPanel, go to File Manager, and navigate to public_html.
    o   Use the **Upload** feature to transfer files directly from your computer.

5. Setting Up the Database on the Server

To deploy your MySQL database, you need to create a new database on the server and import your local database structure and data.

1. **Create a Database**:
    o   In cPanel, go to **MySQL Databases**.
    o   Create a new database and database user. Assign the user to the database with appropriate permissions.

2. **Export and Import the Database**:

o Export your local database as an SQL file using phpMyAdmin or the MySQL command line:

bash

```
mysqldump -u local_user -p local_database > database.sql
```

o In cPanel, open **phpMyAdmin**, select your new database, and use the **Import** tab to upload the SQL file.

o Alternatively, if using a VPS, you can upload the SQL file to your server and run:

bash

```
mysql -u your_database_user -p your_database_name < database.sql
```

6. Configuring Permissions and Security

Securing your PHP application on a live server is crucial. Some key steps include:

1. **File and Directory Permissions**:

   o Ensure sensitive files (e.g., configuration files) have restricted permissions.

   o Standard permissions:

- Folders: 755
- Files: 644

- Command to set permissions (for Linux):

bash

```
sudo find /path/to/your/app -type d -exec chmod
755 {} \;
sudo find /path/to/your/app -type f -exec chmod 644
{} \;
```

2. **Secure Database Access**:
   - Avoid using the root database user for your application; instead, create a dedicated user with limited privileges.
   - Use strong, complex passwords for database users.

3. **Use HTTPS**:
   - If your hosting plan includes SSL, enable HTTPS to encrypt data between the server and client.
   - Many hosting providers offer free SSL certificates through Let's Encrypt.
   - In Apache, configure HTTPS by setting up a virtual host for port 443 and specifying your SSL certificate paths.

7. Configuring DNS and Domain

To make your application accessible via a domain name, configure your domain's DNS settings.

1. **Update DNS Records**:
   o Log in to your domain registrar's control panel (e.g., GoDaddy, Namecheap).
   o Update the **A record** to point to your server's IP address.
   o If using a shared hosting provider, set the nameservers as instructed by the provider.

2. **Verify DNS Propagation**:
   o It may take a few hours for DNS changes to propagate.
   o Use tools like nslookup or online DNS propagation checkers to verify.

8. Final Testing and Troubleshooting

After deploying your application, thoroughly test it to ensure everything works as expected.

1. **Test Key Features**:
   o Test forms, user authentication, and database interactions.
   o Ensure all links and images load correctly.

2. **Check for Errors in Logs**:

- o Review error logs in cPanel or your server's file system to catch any runtime errors.
- o Use tail to monitor error logs in real-time:

bash

```
tail -f /path/to/error.log
```

3. **Optimize Performance**:
   - o Enable caching for static files (CSS, JavaScript) by setting cache headers in .htaccess:

apache

```
<IfModule mod_expires.c>
    ExpiresActive On
    ExpiresByType image/jpg "access plus 1 month"
    ExpiresByType image/jpeg "access plus 1 month"
    ExpiresByType image/png "access plus 1 month"
    ExpiresByType text/css "access plus 1 week"
    ExpiresByType application/javascript "access plus 1 week"
</IfModule>
```

4. **Run Database Performance Checks**:
   - Optimize database queries and indexes, especially if your site is data-heavy.
   - Run ANALYZE TABLE and OPTIMIZE TABLE commands to keep your MySQL tables performing well.

9. Backup and Maintenance

Regular backups and maintenance are crucial to keep your application running smoothly.

1. **Database Backup**:
   - Schedule automated database backups with mysqldump or through cPanel's backup options.
   - Example command:

   bash

   ```
   mysqldump -u user -p database > /path/to/backup.sql
   ```

2. **File Backup**:
   - Create regular backups of your application files using cron jobs or scheduled tasks in cPanel.

3. **Update Software Regularly**:
   - Keep PHP, MySQL, and any dependencies up to date to patch security vulnerabilities.

In this chapter, we covered the process of deploying a PHP and MySQL application to a live server. We discussed choosing a hosting provider, setting up the server environment, configuring your application, uploading files, and managing the database on the server. With these steps, you can launch your PHP application for public access and ensure it's secure and performant. In the next chapter, we'll explore

CHAPTER 20: BEST PRACTICES AND FUTURE TRENDS IN PHP AND MYSQL

1. Clean Code Principles

Writing clean code makes your application easier to understand, debug, and maintain. Here are some best practices for writing clean PHP code:

1. Use Descriptive Naming Conventions

- Use clear, descriptive names for variables, functions, and classes.
- Follow a consistent naming convention (e.g., camelCase for variables and methods, PascalCase for class names).

php

```php
class UserManager {
    private $userDatabase;

    public function getUserById($userId) {
        // Code logic here
    }
}
```

2. Follow DRY (Don't Repeat Yourself) Principles

Avoid duplicating code by creating reusable functions and classes. The DRY principle helps reduce redundancy and improves maintainability.

php

```php
function calculateDiscount($price, $discountRate) {
    return $price - ($price * $discountRate);
}
```

3. Keep Functions Short and Focused

Functions should do one thing well. This makes them easier to test and debug, and it improves code readability.

php

```php
function validateEmail($email) {
    return filter_var($email, FILTER_VALIDATE_EMAIL) !== false;
}
```

4. Use Comments and DocBlocks

Comments should clarify why code exists, not what it does. Use PHPDoc for functions and methods to describe parameters, return values, and potential exceptions.

php

```
/**
 * Calculate the total price with tax.
 *
 * @param float $price The original price.
 * @param float $taxRate The tax rate as a decimal.
 * @return float The total price with tax.
 */
function calculateTotal($price, $taxRate) {
    return $price + ($price * $taxRate);
}
```

5. Follow PSR Standards

PHP Standard Recommendations (PSRs) provide a set of coding standards, such as PSR-1 for basic coding standards and PSR-12 for extended coding style. Using these standards ensures consistency in your codebase.

2. Performance Optimization Tips

Optimizing PHP and MySQL can significantly enhance application speed, improve user experience, and reduce server load.

PHP Optimization Tips

1. **Use Native Functions**: PHP's native functions are often faster than custom implementations. For example, use array_sum() instead of looping through an array to calculate the sum.

2. **Minimize Database Queries**: Avoid repeated database queries. Retrieve data once and store it in variables or arrays if you need to access it multiple times.

3. **Use OpCode Caching**: PHP OpCode caching, like **OPcache**, stores precompiled script bytecode in memory, reducing the need to recompile PHP code on each request.

4. **Avoid Excessive Use of require and include**: Using too many require or include statements can slow down your application. Instead, consider using autoloading for classes.

5. **Optimize Loops**: Minimize operations within loops. For example, move calculations or function calls outside the loop if they do not need to be repeated.

php

```php
$count = count($array);
for ($i = 0; $i < $count; $i++) {
    // Loop logic here
}
```

MySQL Optimization Tips

1. **Index Frequently Queried Columns**: Indexes improve the speed of SELECT queries. Index columns used in WHERE clauses, JOINs, and ORDER BY statements.

sql

```sql
CREATE INDEX idx_user_email ON users(email);
```

2. **Limit Data Retrieved**: Use LIMIT and specific column selection in queries to minimize data transfer.

sql

```sql
SELECT name, email FROM users LIMIT 10;
```

3. **Optimize JOINs and Subqueries**: Use JOINs efficiently by indexing the columns involved and minimizing the number of JOINs in a single query.

4. **Use EXPLAIN to Analyze Queries**: Use EXPLAIN to understand query execution plans and identify slow queries or unnecessary full table scans.

sql

```sql
EXPLAIN SELECT * FROM orders WHERE user_id = 5;
```

5. **Regularly Clean and Optimize Tables**: Use OPTIMIZE TABLE to reduce storage overhead and improve performance.

sql

OPTIMIZE TABLE users;

3. Security Best Practices

Ensuring your PHP application is secure is crucial, as vulnerabilities can expose sensitive data or compromise your system.

1. **Validate and Sanitize Input**: Always validate user inputs and sanitize output to prevent SQL injection and cross-site scripting (XSS).
2. **Use Prepared Statements**: Always use prepared statements for SQL queries to protect against SQL injection.
3. **Hash Passwords**: Use password_hash() and password_verify() to store passwords securely.
4. **Enable HTTPS**: Use HTTPS to encrypt data between the server and client.
5. **Limit Error Messages in Production**: Hide detailed error messages in production to prevent exposing sensitive information.
6. **Implement CSRF Protection**: Protect sensitive actions by using CSRF tokens for forms and AJAX requests.
7. **Use Secure Session Management**: Regenerate session IDs upon login and use session_set_cookie_params to secure session cookies.

4. Future Trends in PHP and MySQL

PHP and MySQL continue to evolve with new features, improvements, and community-driven trends. Here's a look at what the future holds for both technologies:

PHP 8+ and Modern PHP Features

1. **PHP 8.1 and Beyond**: New PHP versions (PHP 8.0 and PHP 8.1) bring features like **JIT (Just-in-Time) Compilation**, **attributes**, **enums**, and **readonly properties**, improving performance and developer productivity.
2. **Typed Properties and Arguments**: The move towards strict typing (introduced in PHP 7) continues, allowing better error detection, enhanced code quality, and better integration with IDEs.
3. **Asynchronous PHP**: Libraries like **Swoole** and frameworks like **ReactPHP** allow for asynchronous programming, which can handle concurrent processes and real-time applications better.
4. **Improved Error Handling and Debugging**: With better error handling, stack traces, and debugging tools, PHP is becoming more robust for enterprise-level applications.

Future Trends in MySQL

1. **JSON and NoSQL Support**: Modern MySQL versions support JSON data types, allowing for flexible data storage formats similar to NoSQL databases. This hybrid model

supports applications that need both relational and document-based data storage.

2. **Improved Replication and High Availability**: Newer MySQL versions have improved replication, clustering, and automatic failover, which enhances data availability for large-scale applications.

3. **MySQL 8 Optimizations**: MySQL 8 introduces features like invisible indexes, window functions, and improved sorting algorithms. These enhancements make MySQL more competitive with other enterprise databases.

4. **Automatic Partitioning and Sharding**: As data grows, partitioning and sharding help distribute data across multiple servers. These features are increasingly supported in MySQL-compatible systems like Amazon Aurora and Google Cloud SQL.

Headless CMS and Microservices Architecture

1. **Headless CMS**: The headless CMS architecture decouples the backend (content management) from the frontend, allowing developers to build frontend interfaces in JavaScript frameworks (e.g., React, Vue) while the backend serves data through an API. PHP frameworks, like **Laravel** with **Laravel Nova**, support this approach, making PHP a popular choice for headless CMS development.

2. **Microservices**: Microservices architecture breaks applications into smaller, modular services that communicate via APIs. PHP can be used in microservices alongside other languages and works well with API-driven architectures.

The Role of PHP and MySQL in Cloud and Serverless Computing

1. **Cloud Integration**: PHP applications are increasingly deployed on cloud platforms like AWS, Google Cloud, and Azure, which offer scalability and managed MySQL databases (e.g., Amazon RDS, Google Cloud SQL). This setup allows for auto-scaling and robust database management.

2. **Serverless PHP**: While serverless architectures are traditionally associated with JavaScript and Python, PHP can also run in serverless environments with solutions like **Bref** on AWS Lambda. Serverless PHP allows you to run functions without managing server infrastructure.

3. **Containerization with Docker**: Docker has become a popular choice for deploying PHP applications due to its consistency across environments. By containerizing PHP and MySQL, developers can ensure the same environment in development, staging, and production.

In this chapter, we explored clean coding principles, performance optimization techniques, security best practices, and emerging trends in PHP and MySQL. By following these best practices and staying aware of new developments, you'll be able to build applications that are scalable, secure, and maintainable.

As PHP and MySQL continue to evolve, integrating these technologies with modern web development practices (like microservices, cloud hosting, and serverless computing) will further expand their role in building high-performance, future-ready applications. Keep learning, adapting, and refining your skills to stay at the forefront of web development with PHP and MySQL!

www.ingramcontent.com/pod-product-compliance
Lightning Source LLC
La Vergne TN
LVHW051320050326
832903LV00031B/3268